40 Days Understanding the Heart and Mind of God

Ernie Pyle
& Rob Sheppard

ISBN 9798561045400

Cover images courtesy of Madison Jobe
Cover by Joleene Naylor

This book is Dedicated to
Sue Pyle
Without Sue there would be no
"Knowing God Ministry"

Special thanks to:
Dian McClain
And
Dona Klein
Who helped bring this project home

Table of Contents

INTRODUCTION
By Ernie Pyle

I know you've got to be curious and asking yourself, "How did these two guys arrive at the desire to write something about which the Bible is silent?" It seems that if God wanted us to know about the forty days in the wilderness, He would have had something to say about it. But, no, nothing is said.

Let me share with you the background that led to this devotional.

I became ill, seriously ill. I debated within myself, "Is this it? Will I make it out of this hospital?" I had to have a heart stent, my kidneys kicked out on me, I was facing dialysis within the next thirty six hours, and my gall bladder was out of whack. All this led me to the possibility that maybe my number may be up.

I was in the hospital fourteen days, and every morning, and several times each day, I prayed, "Father, take care of me; but if You mean for me to go on, get me out of here." I talk pretty openly and honestly with my Father.

Rob Sheppard and I had started a ministry called, "Knowing God Ministry." This ministry took us all over the nation, into Canada, and to Hawaii (suffering for the Lord). I just knew God wanted us to do that, and I believed He wanted me to go on with this ministry and finish it. And sure enough, He got me out and back on my feet.

While I was in the hospital something dawned on me and left me with a question. I started thinking, "God, are you sick and tired of hearing the same prayers over and over from me? You must be bored." In between those prayers I got to thinking about Jesus and His Father in the wilderness for forty days together. What did they talk about? The Bible is silent on that experience, but I figure He never minds my persistent questions, so I didn't believe I was arrogant or irreverent to ask Him, "What did You and Your Son talk about? You've had secret meetings before, and eventually allowed us to know what those meetings were about; how about this meeting?"

I brought my question to my partner in ministry, Rob Sheppard. At first he had a weird look on his face. Probably similar to the look I often had as he desperately tried to teach me Greek II in college. Finally, after a long pause he said, "I never seriously thought about it. Now I'm curious."

That launched it. Here we are today, in our hands is the finished project. Thanks to many helpers. Rob and I are so thankful for Dona Klein and Dian McClain, who tirelessly rewrote and made sense out of our thoughts, put them in order, then typed it all out. From the depths of our hearts, THANK YOU!

This book is an imaginary conversation between Jesus and His Father, asking questions we would ask. The conversation was to give the Son an in-depth look at His Father's heart and mind. Now we invite you to be, as it were, a mouse in the corner with us, eaves dropping on the conversation between Father and Son.

Enjoy your journey!

A FORTY DAY JOURNEY INTO KNOWING THE MIND AND HEART OF OUR HEAVENLY FATHER

John 17:3 "And this is eternal life, that they may know Thee, the only true God and Jesus Christ whom Thou has sent."

INTRODUCTION
By Rob Sheppard

This devotional is an invitation to come with us as we delve into the Word of God to explore His mind and heart. The journey is for forty days

Why forty days? God invited Moses to spend forty days on Mt. Sinai to behold His character. Moses did, and came down with his face aglow. He beheld God's beauty for forty days and He could hardly contain himself as he ran among the children of Israel to share what he saw.

Isaiah and Daniel beheld the beauty of God. Their strength left them because of the wonders of His character, and then they wanted to run among the people to tell what they saw.

Jesus went into the wilderness to pray about His mission. He was shut in with His Father for forty days. He came forth from that, defeated the Devil, and went among the people telling them about His Father.

Jesus, after His resurrection, joined the despondent two men on their journey to Emmaus, and inquired of them why they were so down. They responded, "We thought Jesus was the Messiah, but the leaders killed Him." Notice what Jesus did. He began with Moses and went through all the prophets and told them how all of those stories were about Him, and that what happened to Jesus was all foretold in Scripture. And what was the response from those two men? They said, "Didn't our hearts burn within us as we walked with Him in the way?"

What caused their hearts to burn? It was all the stories

He told them from the Old Testament about Himself.

That is what this forty day journey is all about. It is our belief that during the forty days Jesus spent with His Father, He did what He did in the temple when He was twelve years old. He couldn't stop asking questions of the temple priests. He couldn't stop asking His Father questions. The Father revealed to Him His character.

Ernie was in the hospital wondering what did the Heavenly Father and His Son talk about for forty days? We have no evidence of what they discussed; the Scripture is silent about that conversation. But Ernie imagined, "If they did talk, what did they say?" He shared his questions with me, and I got to thinking "What did they say?"

With no intent to be irreverent, we both came to the same conclusion; "They must have talked about the plan of redemption as revealed in the Old Testament." Frankly speaking, that's the only Scripture available; there was no New Testament; Jesus was the Good News!

So we are inviting you to join us and ask of each story, "What does it tell me about my Father's character?" We wrote the stories as a conversation between the Father and Son. Jesus' comments are in italics. The Fathers' responses are in bold italics. In several places a plain font is used to describe settings and background.

We recommend that you read one story each day for forty days. With each story are a prayer and scripture suggestions for further study. By the time you finish the forty days, it is our prayer that you, too, will declare, "Didn't my heart burn within me as I walked with Him in this journey!" May you run among your friends to tell them about your wonderful Heavenly Father.

PREFACE

In my life, I read and reread the biblical story of Jesus Christ's 40 days and nights in the wilderness many times but not once it entered my mind to ask the question: What was Jesus doing during this time besides praying and simply contemplating His upcoming mission? It was an "aha moment" when Pastor Ernie Pyle shared with me the idea that during these 40 days and nights Jesus was probably discussing and conversing with His Heavenly Father about all kinds of topics starting with Creation and ending with His own, in-person glorious Second Coming. The possibility of these highly plausible conversations not only made sense, but also inspired me with a heartfelt desire to converse more with my Heavenly Father and ask Him all kinds of questions relevant to my personal life and struggles. After all, Jesus Himself encouraged us to do just that (Mark 7:7 NIV). "Ask and it will be given to you; seek and you will find; knock and the door will be open to you."

In our lives, we certainly have more questions than answers. Some of our questions we just dare not ask for fear of embarrassment or simply for a perceived lack of getting real answers. Not so with God. The more we communicate and spend time with God, the closer we get to Him and the more we discover His amazing love for us. We can certainly converse with God the Father, and Jesus, and the Holy Spirit. We might not get exactly what we are looking for, but we will certainly walk away blessed and spiritually satisfied from a conversation with a loving Heavenly Father. No doubt that while He was here among us, Jesus talked a lot with His Heavenly Father. We can do the same.

I have known the authors of this book, Pastor Ernie Pyle and Dr. Rob Sheppard, for 19 years and counting. They have been my friends and mentors through thick-and-thin. I have also been their pastor for most of this time, and have had them engaged in my pastoral ministry in the churches I pastored. When we were together at an Arlington, Texas, church, they started the "Knowing God Ministries" which became a blessing to many churches around the country, and directly to all the churches I pastored since. These men of God have a relationship with the Savior and love people. I am pleased to see that they put this book together to rejuvenate your spiritual life with the Lord. Ask your question, converse with God, ponder on His character; you will be surprised at the answers you get and the blessings that carry you through into His Kingdom.

Oh, and last, but not least, this bible verse comes to mind as I am thinking about my friends, Ernie and Rob. 1 Corinthians 15:58 says, "Therefore, my dear brothers and sisters, be steadfast, immovable, always excelling in the Lord's work, because you know that your labor in the Lord is not in vain."

To the reader: May your 40 Days and Nights with God be a long-lasting blessing!

- Pastor Ion Groza, pastor

Your journey is about to begin. Our recommendation for how to use this book as it was intended, is for you, and perhaps your family, to dedicate the next 40 days to reading one story each day for your worship time. To set the stage for this experience, imagine that you have been given the same opportunity which the prophet Isaiah describes in chapter six of his book. He listened in on a conversation between the Father and His Son, when they were trying to solve the problem of how to convey their message of love to Their children of Israel. They said, "Who can we get to go tell Our children how much we love them?" Isaiah couldn't contain himself when he heard their dilemma. He thrust his arm in the air, waving it back and forth. "Here I am. Send me!"

We pray that is your response. Have a happy journey!

JESUS MEETS HIS FATHER

The sun bore down on Jesus as He was putting the finishing touches on the bridge He was repairing. A group of men were walking together and carrying on an animated conversation, oblivious of the young carpenter. Jesus overheard them talking about a man, thought to be a prophet, preaching and baptizing many people.

Jesus interrupted the conversation and asked *"What is this about a prophet, preaching?"*

"Yes," one of the men responded, "he is near Aenon, about forty miles from here, on the river Jordan. His message is that the time has come. God is sending the Messiah, and that we must be ready by confessing our sins, and being baptized."

Something stirred in the heart of Jesus. He knew His time had come. A very solemn mood came over Jesus as He made His way home to announce to His parents He was leaving and going south to the river Jordan and yet He was not alone. In His mind flooded the texts which He often read:

"A voice is calling out, clear the way for the Lord in the wilderness; make smooth in the desert a highway for our God. Let every valley be lifted up, and every mountain and hill be made low; and let the rough ground become a plain…then the glory of the Lord will be revealed, and all flesh will see it together, for the mouth of the LORD has spoken. (Isaiah 40:3-5)

"Behold, I am going to send My messenger, and He will clear the way before Me. And the Lord, whom you seek, will suddenly come to His temple; and the messenger of the covenant in whom you delight, behold, He is coming, says the LORD of Hosts." (Malachi 3:1)

Not only did He recall all of these scriptures, He also had the ever present question: the God He saw in the Old Testament, in nature, and verified in His experience was vastly different than the God portrayed in the sacrificial system and by the leaders as they read the Old Testament.

God knew the mind and heart of man. He realized man succumbed to the lie told by Satan about God: "God cannot be trusted, He is an angry God, betray or disobey Him, and He will kill you." He also knew the Devil had distorted the way back to God. The Devil's message was "God is angry with man and the only way to appease Him is to follow His rules, perform all of His required rituals, do more good than bad, and perhaps you can earn your way back into His favor."

Jesus knew man would take the information he heard about God, create his own image of God, and then worship that as if it was real, whether it resembled a fish or a bull.

But that is not the character of God that Jesus saw in

Scripture. Jesus' heart burned within Him as He read the Bible. His joy overflowed. He couldn't wait to be fully in His Father's presence.

This was quite the opposite of what He heard from the priests about God being a force in the universe one must come to grips with: so do what He requires to avoid punishment; and by all means avoid His presence, if possible.

Jesus knew the priests created great mountains, impossible valleys, rough, jagged, deserts between man and God; the way to God was impossible. Jesus was to become God's thoughts made audible, and make the way to the Father clear and easy.

As Jesus approached the place where John was baptizing, He saw a crowd of people milling about as sheep in the wilderness. He wanted to hold them, and comfort them. He heard the voice of the Baptist crying out, "Prepare the way for the Lord in your heart, repent and be baptized, every one of you." Jesus made His way to John.

Jesus' and John's eyes met. There was a long silence in John's voice, and a look of amazement on his face, almost disbelief. Then in a loud voice, John cried out, "Behold, the Lamb of God, who will take away the sins of the world!" All the people turned to see who John was talking about.

Jesus stepped into the Jordan river and approached John to be baptized. John began to back up, his eyes wide in disbelief, and he began to bow low. John raised his hand in an effort to stop Jesus and gasped, "No! I need to be baptized by You! I'm not deserving to even remove your shoes." And Jesus said, *"Allow it to be so for now, for We are following the will of My Father."*

When Jesus came forth from the river, the heavens

seemed to open, and through the opening came a dove, a symbol of peace, alighting on His shoulder. And a clear voice, with such pathos of tenderness and love, stated, **"This is My Son, in whom I am well pleased, hear Him."** John and all the people were in awe. What just happened?

Jesus often heard a loving voice in His heart during prayer, or while reading about His Father in the Old Testament, or in nature, but this is the first time He heard it audibly in public.

Jesus walked out of the river and passed through the crowd. He felt compelled to go toward the wilderness. He remembered thinking, *"Why this way, into the desert? The people You sent me to save are back there, by the river. For what reason am I going this way into the desert? What possibly could be there for Me?"*

PRAYER: Father, please help me to grasp the reality of what Jesus was willing to sacrifice in order to come to save me.

Further study: Matthew 4,
Luke 4,
John 1

LOVE IS WHAT
LOVE DOES

As Jesus made His way into one of the most desolate places on earth, something strange began to happen. The forbidden lifeless environment began to disappear. He found Himself enfolded in an atmosphere of pure love and security. Those words he heard on the banks of the Jordan repeated over and over in His mind, **"This is My beloved Son, hear Him."** And yet it seemed a contradiction. *"I am Your Son, and yet are You compelling Me to walk away from the ones I've come to save, and into a wilderness?"* Jesus thought.

It was then Jesus heard that beautiful, assuring voice again. **"Come, My Son, I have something to show You."** In a moment Jesus was swept away into the vast, beautiful universe. He could see the distant stars become beautiful constellations. It was breathtaking! On He went to the most wonderful place.

"This is heaven, this was Your home." Jesus saw the shimmering reflection of the golden city with its streets of gold and precious stones. He saw the inhabitants of that city-mighty, lovely angels. Then He was stunned as He beheld His Father on the throne. It was awesome! The love the angels exhibited while ministering to the Father, and the Father's kind tender response was overwhelming.

Jesus thought, *"Oh, if only the dark, dark earth could behold this, and our lovely heavenly Father, they would all change in a moment."*

The Father, knowing Jesus' thoughts, said, **"Yes, this**

is beautiful and impressive; but remember the one who stood by My side, the covering angel, and a third of this vast throng of angels You see, believed a lie started by that covering cherub. They rebelled and left all of this.

"Love is what love does. I could show them all of this and reveal My power, but what love does in the presence of a sinful world is the only thing that will change the world. If I use the power of this environment, if I use any force, it will never change the heart or condition of man, and it will not make all heaven and eternity safe. Only by love is love awakened. Any other means of force or manipulation will end up creating rebels and an unending line of devils.

"Behold Enoch, Moses, and Elijah! They are here because they saw their condition; they experienced My love, forgiveness, and redeeming grace. They did not believe the devils' lies; they trusted Me. They will be safe throughout eternity!

"You must go back to that dark, forsaken place. You must go to the most sinful, weak, rebellious ones, to the depths of darkness, and bring the light of My forgiveness and redeeming love. Let them know I will do anything, even the sacrifice of Myself or My Son, to bring them home."

"Father, now I understand what You have been telling them all along through the sanctuary and offerings. Daddy, that is the message You have been saying through all the prophets. Father, I now know I will bring them the truth about You, I am to be not only the Messenger, and to demonstrate Your thoughts about sinners, I am to be the full example of what sin, let go, will do, and the length to which You are willing to go in order to provide a way home."

"Yes, Son, that is what must be done. Will you accept that mission?"

Jesus cried out, *"I have come to do Your will. Yes, I will go tell them."*

PRAYER: Father, it overwhelms me to think that Your love is so strong it is even stronger than death: You said You would have died for me, but the greatest, deepest love was to allow Your Son to come. Thank You.

Further study: John 3:11-21

DISCOVERING
HIS MISSION

It had been only a short time since Jesus had come up out of the waters of the Jordon river. The heavens opened up, and the bright image of a Dove had descended upon Him. The sound of those melodious words which came from heaven were still echoing in His Ears: **"This is My Beloved Son, in whom I am well pleased."** This is the second time that the audible connection between heaven and earth was heard; the first time was at His birth when the angelic choir sang, "Glory to God in the highest, peace on earth, and good will toward men."

Jesus was compelled to follow the leading of that Dove into the wilderness; but there was a confused look on His face. So, Jesus did that which He had done His entire life: He found a quiet place, fell to His knees, and began to talk to His Father. *"Daddy, it seems a long time since I first realized I was put on this earth for a very special purpose. I believe I followed Your will by staying with My family and doing daily what was before Me. When I heard of John the Baptist preaching and announcing that the Messiah was coming, I realized He was talking about Me.*

"I knew You were with Me throughout My life, and leading Me by Your Spirit. I am willing to follow wherever You lead Me, but why into the wilderness? I was excited to begin preaching right away to that group on the banks of the Jordan, but then I felt led by Your Spirit to go in the opposite direction, into a barren desert. What is it

that You want Me to do?"

Jesus felt the presence of His Father, as if He was enfolded by His presence. The starkness of the desert faded away, and the brightness of His Father surrounded Him. His Daddy began to speak. ***"Jesus, You are correct; from the moment You were conceived inside Your precious Mother, I was with You. Your birth, and all of the stories You have heard and read in Scripture have created some questions in Your mind. You have been curious about them since You first began asking about them when You were twelve years old, and You questioned the leaders of the church. I want to talk with You so those questions can be answered. You can understand how all of this began from the beginning of time, and understand Your mission.***

"What You are beholding and experiencing today is not the way it always has been. From the beginning of time You have always been with Me. There was peace in heaven; not a blight in the entire universe. We created this world together. The entire heavenly host was fashioned by Your own hand. All was glorious; that is, until the most beautiful created being was lifted up by his own pride. You made him so wonderful, and You and he were such good friends."

Jesus was silent as all of what His Daddy had said dawned fully upon Him. His mind flooded with the description He had read in the Scriptures about the Messiah. He, as the King of Kings, Lord of Lords, the Mighty God, had been standing by His Father from all eternity. With every being created He took it upon Himself to make sure that they knew and understood the mind and the heart of God. So closely He aligned Himself with the creation, that they saw Him as their friend.

"As the Light Bearer, Jesus, You went throughout the universe spreading the beams of love to all, and

made sure all knew they were Our friends. The one who stood nearest to Our throne, who was adored by other angels, became envious, and jealous of the praise they gave You. And he, lifted up by his own beauty, wanted to be equal with, and seen as God. He was our most trusted, and wonderful friend. How you labored with Him and yet his thoughts blossomed into distrust of us.

"Several times You accomplished bringing Lucifer back from the precipice he was about to plunge over. He sowed discontent among all the heavenly host, and cast doubts in their minds about Our love for them. He drew a third of the citizens of heaven away. Then the plan We devised from the foundation of the universe had to be put in place. We had to pursue the heavenly host and try to save them from destroying themselves; for they did not realize that separation from Us as the source of life, would only end in them destroying themselves." Tears were flowing from His Daddy's eyes.

"That rebellion spread to earth, Your most beautiful creation. Look at the results in the planet, and in Our children." The Father groaned because of the pain the rebellion caused His children. *"You have heard the twisted ideas Satan has sown in the minds of Our children. Your mission, My Son, is not just to tell them of Our love, You must live it out in Your life. Only by love demonstrated will love and trust be created. We must pursue them, and let them know there is a way back. Tell them they are forgiven, and that they have life, and their love and life will grow if only they will put their trust in Us."*

Daddy and His Son stood embracing; their bodies trembling from the thought of what was ahead of them. *"Go."* The Father cried to His Son. *"Tell them about Our love, and bring as many as will accept Our gift back into Our arms of love. And I will be with You every step of the way."*

PRAYER: Oh, Father, help me to realize Your love for me, and the great price You and Your Son have paid to bring us life eternal. Teach me how to trust and to love.

Further study: Isaiah 53,
Psalm 40,
Hebrew 10

ABRAHAM, GOD'S FRIEND

Not all the time Jesus remained in the Father's presence did They talk. Often They sat together in silence absorbing the infinite love They had for One another. The silence was broken when Jesus asked, *"Daddy, tell Me about Your friendship with Abraham. Your children on earth have claimed him as their father; much of what they do in their religious practice surrounds the things Abraham did. I want to know about Him."*

"Ah, yes. Where do I start? Much of our time could be spent on telling the stories about My old friend. I have to be so cautious with My children; they have the habit of taking things, and places, and people, and even events, and making them objects of worship, instead of looking at them as the means I use to convey how much I love them, and what I do to reveal My heart to them.

"I believe it is important to know a little about Abraham's background. He lived at the time near the end of Noah's life. Abram, as he was first known, often talked to Noah and his sons. They shared with him the stories about the people before the flood who were giants in stature and intellect. All of their energy was spent continually obsessed with evil.

"I had to put an end to their destroying themselves. Before I did, however, I gave Noah the promise of a seed who would crush out evil. It appeared to the unfallen angels in heaven that the

Devil had won the great controversy. But, I had to let them see that what I told Adam and Eve at the fall was true; that is, the wages of sin ends naturally in death. Then I told Abram about the Seed, about You, Jesus, that You would crush the serpent's head, and You would make a way to restore in man the image he once had.

"Abram saw that much of the evil that was before the flood was gaining hold again. My friend pled with Me to send that Seed. The time was not right for You to come into the world. I could describe many of the stories about Abram, but I had two major things I wanted the world to see through Abram's life. One thing I wanted to show was what would happen in the life of one who puts his trust in Me, and the other thing was how I could reveal My mind and heart of love for My children.

"Early in Abram's life I gave him the promise that through him the Seed would come. I visited him one night, and I asked him to come out of his tent, and to count all the stars in heaven. I assured him the Seed would come through him, and his children would be as great in number as the stars in the heavens. Abram gasped and asked how that could be, because he didn't have any children, and he knew Sarah could not even produce one. I told him I knew that, but I promised he would have a child, and through him the Seed would come.

"Now here is the key to his entire life: Abram said, 'Father, I TRUST YOU.' That is the key moment in any man's life. It was at that moment I counted Abram righteous, and changed his name to Abraham: Father of a Nation. Everything which happened after *that statement of faith, of trust, was the result of Me working in him, to do for him what he could not do for himself. Do You understand he was complete at that moment of surrender?*

"Every step of the way for the rest of Abraham's life it was Me working in him. The climax of his life was the moment he was willing to do My bidding to offer his son as a sacrifice. You know, Son, I would never have had him kill his son; I just had to get him to the place that I could let him see into My heart to see what it was like for Me to sacrifice My Son for all men. He was the first man who trusted Me enough to be My friend, and who could lose sight of himself long enough that I could fully open My heart and mind to help him see the sacrifice I am willing to make to bring My children home to Me.

"My friend and I sat on top of that mountain together, and I showed him the future before him. He saw Your day, and he was glad. Then I showed him the future when all will be restored to heaven once again. It is through You that all of this is possible."

The Father and Son stood embracing each other. Jesus said, *"I will reveal Your heart and mind again, Father, for the entire universe to behold Your love."*

PRAYER: Thank you, Father, for the insight into what You did for Abraham, and what You will do for me.

Further Study: Genesis 15-22

BEHOLD
THE LAMB OF GOD

There was silence between the Father and His son. Throughout all of their conversations the stark reality of why Jesus came to earth had not been fully addressed until now.

"Father, from a child on My mother's knee, and when I questioned the leaders of the temple when I was twelve, and then as I was growing up, I pondered what Isaiah had to say about Me and My mission. I did not fully understand until now; I am that Lamb. Isaiah was talking about Me."

"From the foundation of the universe We, the Godhead, had to find a way to save Our children in case sin did arise. We knew any words of caution would never fully explain what sin would do. We had to do all We could to restore Our children if it did happen. We would have to demonstrate for all to see that sin, let go, would kill the sinner, kill the creation, and if possible, try to kill the Creator. We had to let the full effects of sin be carried out to the end. Had We allowed the effects of sin to happen right away, no one would understand and it would look like We were punishing for sin. We can only operate the universe on the principle of love and never use force."

"Father, Now I understand the words I memorized when just a child. Now it all makes sense:"

Who has believed what he has heard from us?
And to whom has the arm of the Lord been revealed?

For He grew up before him like a young plant,
And like a root out of dry ground;
He had no form or majesty that we should look at Him,
And no beauty that we should desire Him.
He was despised and rejected by men,
A man of sorrows and acquainted with grief;
And as One from whom men hide their faces
He was despised, and we esteemed him not.

Surely He has borne our griefs
And carried our sorrows;
Yet we esteemed Him stricken,
Smitten by God, and afflicted.
But He was pierced for our transgressions;
He was crushed for our iniquities;
Upon Him was the chastisement that brought us peace,
And with His wounds we are healed.
All we like sheep have gone astray;
We have turned…every one…to his own way;
And the Lord has laid on Him
The iniquity of us all.

He was oppressed, and he was afflicted,
Yet he opened not His mouth;
Like a lamb that is led to the slaughter,
And like a sheep that before its shearers is silent,
So He opened not His mouth.
By oppression and judgment He was taken away;
And as for his generation, who considered
That He was cut off out of the land of the living,
Stricken for the transgression of My people?
And they made His grave with the wicked
And with a rich man in His death,

Although He had done no violence,
And there was no deceit in His mouth.

Yet it was the will of the Lord to crush Him;
He has put Him to grief;
When His soul makes an offering for guilt,
He shall see His offspring; He shall prolong His days;
The will of the Lord shall prosper in His hand.
Out of the anguish of His soul He shall see and be satisfied;
By His knowledge shall the righteous One, My servant,
Make many to be accounted righteous,
And He shall bear their iniquities.
Therefore I will divide him a portion with the many,
And He shall divide the spoil with the strong,
Because He poured out His soul to death
And was numbered with the transgressors;
Yet He bore the sin of many,
And makes intercession for the transgressor.'
"I will go, Father. I must go to seek and to save all who will come to Me. I know You will walk with Me through the valley of the shadow of death. I WILL BRING THEM HOME!"

PRAYER; Thank You, Father, for what You have provided, and for Your Son coming to bring us Home to You. Thank You for offering us the power to become the redeemed sons and daughters of God.

Further Study: Isaiah 53

DAVID

"**B**ut you have not been like my servant David, who kept My commands and followed Me with all his heart, doing only what was right in My eyes."

Has this Bible verse ever confounded you, especially after reading David's Bible-recorded shenanigans? But, those are God's words, and God doesn't lie. Let's see if we can discover how David…shepherd, poet, song writer, slayer of lions and giants, king, repentant sinner, and worship leader extraordinaire…followed God.

"You know, Jesus, I don't have favorites among My children, but it sure was interesting watching David mature in Our relationship. He began as a boy shepherd. Some might think it inconsequential; but that very upbringing, away from the lures of the city…why, Jesus, I can't tell you how many hours we chatted under the stars, his soft music serenading the sheep to sleep. David's character was cemented during those long, lonely hours of obedience. Yes, he was an unlikely candidate to be king. Samuel went through seven older brothers before seeking out David; but, I told Samuel not to make judgment on what he saw, for I always look at the heart…and nothing else."

"Father, all of heaven grabbed ringside seats for David's encounter with the Philistine giant, Goliath. Even as his own brothers mocked him, David turned to the crowd and gave You the glory. I can see how David's dependence on You in the solitary hills

of Bethlehem fed and watered his soul…even as he fed and watered his sheep. Savage beasts were no match for him, and neither was Goliath."

"In succeeding years, David joined King Saul's army, and tremendous battle victories led Saul to regret promoting him. Eventually, Saul ordered David killed; but even in the wilderness, while on the run, David remained loyal to Me and the king I had chosen."

"Father, I see how faithful David was to You, consulting your wisdom before all his decisions; but there came a time when David faltered. You specifically told him not to number his army and he disobeyed. Why did you give him those instructions?"

"Jesus, David had always depended on Me for his success, not on the number of men in his army. That made no difference at all, and he knew it. Now, all of a sudden, David wanted to know how many soldiers he had accumulated! Satan looks for any weakness in My children, and he convinced David that his success was his own doing. Through the prophet Nathan, I broke the news to David that he wouldn't be able to build my temple after all. This consequence was especially heartbreaking for him, and for Me."

"David was to battle again in his relationship with You when he was smitten with Bathsheba. Trying to walk off insomnia, King David was pounding the pavement of the palace roof when he looked down to see a beautiful woman bathing, and he wanted her. David didn't turn to You, or even give a second thought; but immediately sent his men to seek her identity."

"Jesus, when a child of mine strays from My side, Satan plunges in so quickly. David should have been out fighting battles as I had instructed him to do; but here he was, and the temptation was too great without

Me. Again, I sent the prophet Nathan to rebuke David by telling him a story about a rich man who took a poor man's only sheep to feed his guest. David was so angry, but when Nathan explained the rich man in the story was David himself, he admitted his sin immediately and wrote one of the most beautiful Psalms in the Bible. He could really write!"

"Yes, Father, David used his gifts to honor You and bless others. What joy he exhibited when he praised Your name for all to see! What lessons to be learned as he turned to You!"

"David's confession was immediate and sincere, Jesus. I so longed to save him from further sadness, but breaking My law of love brings consequences not only upon the sinner, but those caught in the web of deceit. Yes, tremendous lessons are learned in humbly accepting consequences for one's behavior."

"Father, why do Your children choose to leave Your side when the price is so severe? David lost his own son, and future sons caused him exceeding pain. How did you look at David knowing the future ahead?"

"Jesus, when a sinner turns to Me in repentance, that person is forgiven immediately. I no longer see the sin. I treated David as if he had never left My side. When I looked at David, I saw who he would become by staying close to Me. I love My children so. David repented and moved on. I forgive and move on. David honored Me, and his story will help mankind through the ages to know that there is nothing anyone can do to sever the love ties I have with all of My children. Oh, the stories they will tell one day to the whole Universe!"

All God wants is for us to come home.

PRAYER: I pray that we will see the goodness of God, because all He sees is the goodness in us.

Further Study: I Kings 14:8,
Psalms 51

CAN I REALLY
TRUST YOU?

"Father, coming into Your presence and experiencing Your glory makes the world I'm in seem so dark. It seems that if the world could behold, just for a minute, what I am seeing and experiencing in Your presence, there would be no questions left to ask. Beholding You and the wonderful heavenly world would convict anyone to want to go there."

As Jesus was basking in His Father's presence and envisioning the glorious, dazzling world about His Father, He noticed all the beautiful angelic host; it took His breath away. *"Oh,"* He thought, *"if only the people on earth where I am could see the reality of an existence such as this. If only they knew what it would be like to be surrounded by the safety and love of My Father!"*

"I can't help but notice Your reaction to what You see. You believe seeing the heavenly beauty would surely convince anyone to do all he could to be here? If it was that simple and easy, I would make it so. But I want You to realize that at one time the earth was perfect. The world You are in was once just as beautiful as this heavenly place. When We created the earth it was a reflection of heaven. It was beautiful beyond belief. The garden We made for the first parents, Adam and Eve, was especially beautiful. Yet, being in the midst of it, they were convinced by Satan that I could not be trusted.

"Remember, Satan, once called Lucifer, stood in Our very presence, and was Your very best friend and

yet he began to mistrust. He had everything possible, excelled in beauty beyond what You see in the heavenly host, and yet he fell and turned against Us."

"How can that be?"

"Unbelievable, isn't it?   Lucifer was surrounded by beauty. Adam and Eve could not have had a more beautiful environment; they wanted for nothing, and yet they chose to distrust. It's not the beauty of the place You are in, it's what is in the heart and the mind of the person which makes all of the difference. Heaven can be in the heart of the person even though they exist in that dark place You are in.   Remember, when We created the universe We wanted beings with whom We could interact and enjoy mutual friendship. We insisted they would have total freedom, and We would be bound together by mutual love and trust. We would have it no other way.

"Now Son, do You comprehend Your mission? The real question has been, 'if God could be dropped into the middle of all that sin and rebellion, what would He be like?' This is why You are in their midst as IMMANUEL, God with us."

"Father, I have a question about Moses. I remember reading about an event in his life which surely could have created distrust."

"Are you referring to the striking of the rock to get water for My children? And then how I refused to let him take the children into the promised land, even though he had lived such an exemplary life and begged Me to let him lead them in?"

"Yes. He did such a small thing, just one time, and no matter how he pled, You would not let him lead the children into the promised land.

"Daddy, I trust You. But one could believe that one closest to

You has to be more and more perfect, that he has to obey everything perfectly, and if he makes a mistake one time, it's over."

"Let me explain: Moses had serious questions also. But as he talked to Me, he realized what he had done. The children of Israel could have gone straight into the Promised Land from Egypt, but they mistrusted Me. I led them into the desert to teach them of My love. Moses realized I had to give them further evidence as a basis for their trust in Me. He understood I needed to give them assurance that I could be trusted. I wanted them to see that I was not angry with them for grumbling; I gladly supplied all their needs. Moses knew that by his gesture he conveyed the wrong message. The children of Israel viewed Me as harsh, judgmental, and severe. That was exactly what the Devil said about Me. Moses felt shame and realized that the people looked to him as My spokesperson. Moses knew I was not angry with him, I was his Friend. He understood what I did for him. When it came time for the children to go into the Promised Land, I led him to the mountaintop. I showed him their future and promised I would not leave them. I laid him to rest in a grave. Then I raised him from the dead and brought him here to be with Me. That's what a friend would do.

"You, Jesus, are to do what I wanted Moses to do: to make plain, and sure, what I am like. Jesus, that is Your mission. Your task is to go among the people as their Friend to tell the magnificent story that God is love, and that I do not want any one of My children to destroy himself by separating from Me."

PRAYER: Oh, Father! Now I see that from start to

finish, it's not about me and my performance. It's about You and Your trustworthiness and Your faithfulness; for it's You Who works in me both to will and to do Your good pleasure.

Further Study: Numbers 20:1-13

ELIJAH

Have you ever run from God? Did God have to come to you? He will, you know…every time. Let's look at the life of Elijah, prophet to the ten Northern tribes of Israel during the reign of Ahab. Remember Ahab? He had done a fantastic job of leading the children of Israel into idolatry. So God sent the prophet Elijah to warn Ahab that a drought was coming.

"Jesus, King Ahab's rule had led My children so far away from Me. What could I do to get their attention? I decided to send a drought to destroy their beautiful gardens of worship to Baal. Ahab didn't take kindly to Elijah's warning, so I hid Elijah by a brook and the ravens fed him. I waited three long years, but to no avail. Ahab became even more evil, killing many of My prophets, and the idol worship continued with fervor."

"Father, why would Israel worship a piece of wood, when the Creator of the very tree that provided the wood was appealing lovingly for their hearts? Why wouldn't they listen?"

"Jesus, sometimes man travels down a road for so long that eventually the return is obscured. This was Israel's problem; but, I wasn't about to give up. I told Elijah to challenge the king to a very interesting test that pitted his gods against Elijah's God. Ahab was to slay a bull to sacrifice to Baal while his 450 priests sang and danced and worshipped. Meanwhile, Elijah was to prepare the other bull. The true God would honor only one sacrifice by sending fire from heaven. Everyone agreed!"

"I can just imagine the scene, Father. All of the people gathered,

the hundreds of priests calling out for Baal to answer. Much would be determined that day."

"Yes, the land was scorched and dry. The priests were heavily exhausted after the morning and afternoon passed with no sign in sight. Then Elijah determined to make My case even stronger, He instructed the people to pour water on the altar he had built, enough that it filled a trench around the altar. Oh, bless that Elijah! Then he prayed. Jesus, I sent the hottest fire to burn up the altar, the sacrifice, the stones…even the standing water. It was the greatest display of fireworks ever experienced on Mount Carmel!"

What do we think of Elijah? Two thumbs up?! He courageously confronted the king. He dared 450 priests of Baal, trusting that God had his back. He ordered the slaughter of Baal's prophets, and then predicted rain. One minute he's on top of the world…the next, fleeing Jezebel who was filled with revenge. Poor Elijah. Our natural tendency would be to exclaim, "Buck up, man? God was with you when you announced the drought. He was with you on the Mount. NOW you run and hide?" But our words are not God's words.

"Elijah had done all I asked, Jesus. We were a great team! I wasn't about to let a little discouragement cloud our victory, and so I followed Elijah on his forty-day journey. I cared and provided for him. I strengthened him. I never left his side. Finally, he told me what was on his heart. Oh, I already knew, but had been waiting so patiently to hear from Elijah himself. He was hurting and I came to him, not in a great wind or an earthquake, but in a still, small voice. We reasoned together, and Elijah got himself straightened around. He agreed to go back and anoint his successors.

"Sometimes My children do get discouraged,

Jesus. Satan uses this tool aggressively. But I have overcome the world, and I will guide My children back to My arms. After a mountaintop experience, it is especially important for them not to take their eyes off Me. How quickly My children can stumble and tumble when they allow Satan to register even a seed of doubt! I can see far into the future…the end from the beginning, in fact…and I have already provided for My children before the need is even anticipated."

Elijah was a great man of God. God didn't forsake him and He will never forsake us. Elijah retraced his steps, but this time with purpose. He found his successor, Elisha, plowing in a field. Always be on the look-out for people to mentor and take your place. It is up to the older, experienced leaders to train and support the younger leaders and establish their commitment.

"Jesus, you know from history that Elijah was taken to heaven. Some question why I would translate Elijah, especially after his bouts of depression. The struggle to be perfect is so real for My children. I wish they wouldn't focus on that because I have never asked for perfection. Someday, all those who know Me and hear My voice will be translated. Perhaps I just wanted to give My children a taste of what that will be like, and show them that I keep My word! It is true that Elijah's successor was a great prophet. Why wasn't he taken instead? Well, that discussion we will leave for another hour, Jesus. Let's enjoy the sunset together."

PRAYER: Father may I have the walk with You as Elijah did.

Further Study: I Kings 16-19,
II Kings 2

ELISHA

Elijah was instructed to return from Horeb and anoint two kings before finding his successor, Elisha. He had emptied his heart to God, and with renewed confidence began his return journey from the cave. God was leading this prophet as he found Elisha plowing in a field behind his family's twelve yoke of oxen.

"Father, why didn't You take Elisha to heaven?"

"Elisha came from a wealthy family, Jesus. They owned a great expanse of land, crops, money…but when called to follow in Elijah's footsteps, Elisha didn't question his response. 'Let me go home to kiss my mother and father,' he quickly answered. Then, Elijah asked a second time to make sure of Elisha's commitment, and this time he responded by burning the plowing equipment and butchering the oxen, thus severing ties to his former life. Some might think this a hasty decision, Jesus; but, I had had my eye on Elisha for quite some time. I knew his heart. He was ready to become the servant of Elijah."

Elijah continued to serve God, and one day a company of prophets approached Elisha to inquire if he knew Elijah was going to heaven that very day. Yes, Elisha did know. Elijah had already been given instructions to go to Bethel and the Jordan; and Elisha was admonished to stay behind, but Elisha refused to be separated from his beloved teacher.

"That very day, Jesus, Elijah struck the Jordan River with the same cloak he had wrapped around

Elisha when they first met, and the two walked arm-in-arm across dry ground. What an amazing experience to share together! Elisha went on to become a great prophet with a perfect ministry. He did a fantastic job with the school of prophets. I was so proud of the way he continued on after Elijah was gone. There was no jealousy. He never wavered in his walk with Me. Did you know, Jesus, that Elisha was the last known person to cure a leper...until You cured one?

"Elisha could have thrown a fit and pouted about being left behind. He could even have pointed out Elijah's ministry mistakes. He didn't. He asked Elijah for a double portion of his spirit, and calmly and reverently walked by Elijah's side until, suddenly, Elijah was lifted into the sky. What a scene! What a memory!"

"Yes, Father, Elisha had a tremendous ministry, but then a lingering disease. His last years were painful. I wonder if people who read about these two prophets think it was unfair to take one, and not the other?"

"Jesus, I get asked that question so many times every day. It is an agonizing question. 'Why, God? Why did you allow this to happen? Why did you allow her son to live, and take mine?' If You look throughout history, Jesus, You will see that so many of My followers did not have a tremendous ending to their lives. My plan is unfathomable, but one day all will see and understand My ways. Life on earth is precious. My every thought and action is guided by love and My desire to have as many of My children with Me as possible., Sometimes, I know it is a small consolation, but I have promised My children that I *will never bring upon them more than they can handle. I Love them so.*

"There is One who willingly will go to the cross, Jesus. He won't deserve that death. I pray that My beloved children will trust Me and understand that I do not ask anything of them that I have not already asked of Myself."

PRAYER: Father help me to have the courage and trust of Elisha in my life as I face the ups and downs.

Further study: 2 Kings 2:11-16
2 Kings 4,5,6

IT'S ALL ABOUT BEHOLDING-NOT DOING

"*Oh Father, how my heart hurts! As I have read the Bible over and over, the conclusion I have come to is vastly different than what the teachers are telling Your people. I have read the opposite of what is being told.*"

"**What have You concluded, Son?**"

"*Several things have appeared obvious to Me. One is that every story is about You; from the most insignificant, small story, to the greatest of all, it is about You!*"

"**Tell Me Son, how You see this is so.**"

"*Well, next, I realize that few men in the stories I have read about, realized You were telling the stories about how their belief in a lie about You led them to distrust. In those stories You were revealing the truth about Your heart and mind. You were telling them that You are worthy of their trust.*

"*The enemy has led them to believe the story is about them and their failings. He told them of Your anger and abandonment of them. They think the only way back is to pile up exactions and requirements that they must do to appease Your anger in order to bring You back to them.*

"*Few, Father, have given thought to the suffering that sin has caused to Your heart. Their eyes are blinded and their senses are dulled to the fact of the pain that sin, from its very inception, has brought to your heart, My Creator.*

"*Father, every departure from right, every deed of cruelty, every failure of man to receive Your marvelous gift of salvation, and power to resist believing the lies about You, brought You grief.*

"*When Israel suffered from the calamities which came upon them because of separation from You, they were subjugated and imprisoned by their enemies which resulted in cruelties and death. How Your soul was grieved because of their misery! In their affliction You were afflicted, and You bore them up and carried them in all the days of old!"*

The Father moved closer and embraced the sobbing body of His Son. He said in almost a whisper, ***"Oh, how it pains My heart to think My children hold in their heart the thought that I could abandon them; or to think that I was angry at them just for being in a world separated from Me, and that I would punish them for that."***

The Father wept.

After a long pause of silence, the Holy Spirit cried out with groanings which cannot be uttered, and the entire creation groaned and travailed in pain and sympathy for the heart of the Infinite Father . As the three of Them beheld the misery contained in this fallen world they realized that, if sinners beheld the misery, they would be crushed by the enormity and awfulness of it. And yet, the Creator of this world beholds and carries it all!

Finally, Jesus speaks out with determination, *"I must go and tell them the truth about You; for only by beholding You, can the world be changed."*

PRAYER: Open my eyes that I may see a love stronger than death, and to realize You will let nothing stop You from loving me.

Further study: Proverbs 3:3,
Jeremiah 31:32,
Ezekial11:19 & 36:26,
Ephesians 1:9-10 &15-23,
Colossians 1:19-20,
Hebrews 8:10&10:16

IF LOVE IS THE BASIS
OF THE UNIVERSE, WHY LAWS?

"Father, Your love and kindness overwhelm Me; the reality of Your love is not what I heard from the religious leaders. How can they be so wrong? All of the laws and ceremonies described by Moses are taken by the religious leaders, and then they add laws upon laws, and restrictions upon restrictions until Your children are overwhelmed. The leaders force all of these laws upon Your children, using threats of punishment, or even death, if their demands are not followed. So why are there laws in the first place? How can the leaders do this? They have blinded men and shut out the beauty of Who You are! They don't even do what they demand of the people. It is like they think the laws will ensure their salvation."

"Remember, Son, the one who was once Lucifer, the bearer of light, has become Satan, the liar, the accuser, the slanderer, the angel of darkness. His goal is to hide from the entire universe of unfallen beings Who I am. He distorts truth, and creates fear and reasons to distrust. And he uses religion to do it.

"Your mission, as the Light of the world, is to dispel the darkness by admitting light through Your words and works, to let them know what is in My mind and My heart. For You to understand this I must take You back to describe where much of the confusion lies. Remember when Joseph was sold into slavery and taken to Egypt?"

"Yes."

"Well, My intent was that as Joseph, and later his

family, lived among the Egyptian people, they would be living, loving examples of My love. They eventually failed. Their failure resulted in enslavement. My plan was for them to lead Egypt to become My children, too."

"Now I see. You wanted them, and the universe, to grasp that all the laws are merely promises of what they would become, and that if they severed themselves from the Source of life, the natural results would be that they would bring suffering and death upon themselves."

"Yes! I gave them the promise earlier that their failures would happen, but that I would come and deliver them. I wanted to demonstrate that I would not abandon them, that My power would deliver both them and the Egyptians. I hoped My kindness would convert all of them, but it didn't happen that way. Oh, it hurt Me as I toppled every one of their gods, hoping they would see. But they did not. I finally laid the glory of Egypt in the dust and delivered My children."

"Wait a minute, if that is true then there would not have been a need for an army? And if it is true, then all the books describing Your laws and ceremonies, and the wanderings of Israel, would not have been necessary?"

"That's correct. My children would have been converted by beholding My kindness and experiencing My power to do for them what they could not do for themselves. They would have understood that the only law of the universe is to do right because it is right. They would see the natural consequence which follows every action. I don't punish them. They suffer the consequences of their actions."

"This is amazing, Father. All those promises contained in the Ten Commandments, and scattered throughout the five books of

Moses, are just that? A description of what the people would be like if they accepted those promises?"

"Yes. First, I had to give detailed information of what it would look like if they followed Me, and lay out what would happen naturally if they didn't. Secondly, I wanted them to know that they could learn and follow every law to the letter, but that would not produce any righteousness in them. In fact, it would only produce righteous-acting, unchanged sinners, rebels, if you will, just like their father the Devil. I laid it all out for them and their response was 'All You have said, we will do.' Then I had to let them experience the consequences of their actions."

"And it didn't take long. In less than forty days they had thrown it all aside. They wanted to go back to Egypt."

"Yes, it was after they realized they could not produce righteousness by their own efforts that I took Moses back up the mountain, and at his request, revealed My character to him. This is what the entire essence of religion is all about. Knowing Me, and letting Me into their lives, is what brings change, and recreates in the life of man the image of God I first created in Adam and Eve."

"Now I understand another thing. When Moses experienced the insight into Your heart, he pled with You to let him rush down the mountain to tell the children about Who You are, and that You would be with them as they made their way into the promised land. Moses' face was shining as a result of hearing You and being with You. It shocked Me to hear of their reaction. The children begged Moses to cover his face; they could not bear Your glory. They also begged him not to let You speak to them. They just wanted Moses to talk to You and then convey to them what You said.

"How sad it is, that after witnessing the deliverance from Egypt,

after experiencing all the provisions and protection You provided for their journey, and after seeing the miraculous display of the announcement from Mt. Sinai, most of them did not believe. What else could You have done for Your children?"

PRAYER: Oh, my Father, please, as You did for Moses, reveal Your character of love to me. Please enter my heart, and walk with me in my daily life, that my life may be an appeal to others to follow You.

Further study: John 3&14-17

ESTHER

"*Father, I notice an interesting thing when I read the story of Esther.*"
"What is that, Jesus?"
"*Your name is never mentioned in the story. Please share with Me about Esther.*"

"For several years I sent prophet after prophet to warn My wayward children of Israel that their continued rebellion would bring dire consequences. I even told them that they would go into captivity in Babylon. But they refused to listen. I removed My hedge of protection and the Assyrians swept in and took them to Babylon as slaves."

"*Father, I remember that You didn't leave them without hope.*"

"Right. I told them through Jeremiah that they would only be captive for 70 years and that a man named Cyrus would let them return to Jerusalem, their home.

"When Cyrus gave the decree that My people could return home, about 500,000 of My people felt comfortable and stayed in Babylon."

"*Father, that's unbelievable? How did You feel?*"

"I was disappointed but I loved them as much as I did My children who came home. I was going to take care of them.

"There was a man named Haman who hated the Jews. He was looking for any excuse to kill My Jewish children.

"Then there was My faithful servant, a man named

Mordecai. He had a cousin named Esther. Esther was a very beautiful girl who won a beauty contest to become King Xerxes' queen.

"One day Mordecai refused to bow to Haman. This was just the excuse Haman needed. Haman had tremendous influence over the King. He convinced the King that the Jews were going to cause trouble, and that they should be killed.

"Jesus, one thing You must understand is that <u>I meet people where they ar,</u> and I can only work with what I have.

"When the plot to kill the Jews was found out, Mordecai went to Esther and reminded her that she had come to the kingdom for a reason at this time.

"Esther risked her life to get to the King and tell him of Haman's plot. The king saw the error of his decisions in allowing Haman to kill the Jews. The Jews were protected. Haman was hanged on the gallows he had built to hang Mordecai. King Xerxes praised the Jews.

" I was able to protect My people through Mordecai and a beauty queen."

"Father, I know even though Your Name was not mentioned in the story, obviously You were more interested in protecting the children You love than getting the credit."

PRAYER: Father, thank You. Even when I make a bad decision, You are still in love
with me.

Further study: Book of Esther

ABRAHAM

"Father, You and Abraham were special together. He trusted You so completely that he placed his treasured son's life in Your hands. Satan twisted that story to portray You as a God Who tests His children to prove them worthy or perhaps to set them up for failure. Why would You need to test mankind when You know every heart's secret?"

"It is true, Jesus, that the Adversary often uses this story to confuse My children; however, nothing is hidden from My sight. I know every intricate and intimate detail, even the very number of hairs on their head (Jeremiah 1:5 NIV). **Certainly, there are no surprises. Now, I do test My children from time to time, but the circumstances are always for their edification. Pulling aside the curtain helps them appreciate the present, and remember the past. We become one."**

The nighttime stars overhead spoke of the majesty of God's design, and as Jesus relaxed in His Father's company, He pursued this most delicate idea of God testing His children.

"Father, Abram became Abraham, father of many, and the covenant You made provided him a promised heir and descendants as countless as the stars in the night sky. By the way, Father, the stars are incredible tonight. Their beauty makes Me think that Abraham probably never looked up at the night sky the same again without Your promise ringing in his ears.

"After You declared Abram righteous for believing You would provide him a son, he certainly made some questionable choices, didn't

he? Further, his wife, Sarah, seemed to think You could not be trusted to carry out Your promise. Quite impatiently, she engineered a plan...and Abram went along."

"You are correct, Jesus...about the stars illuminating the universe tonight. This is just the beginning of the beauty I yearn to share with mankind. Oh, sometimes I get as impatient as Sarah.

But You are right...right away Abram began to meddle in My business. In this, however, he was typical of all My children. Throughout history, mankind has struggled with letting Me be God. Because of this interference, Abram experienced many hills and valleys. 'The righteous will fall, but I am right there to help them when they turn to Me' (Prov. 24:16 NIV). **I am always preparing My children for the next step."**

"In time, Father, Isaac was born, and his aged mother laughed with joy! Why, that's the meaning of Isaac's name isn't it...he laughs? She was so happy, she couldn't stop laughing. Father, I pray that the miracle You performed for Sarah encourages other childless women."

There would come a serious day, a day when I would ask Abraham to take his only son and sacrifice him. The Bible says: 'God tested Abraham' (Gen 22:1), **but I had laid the groundwork. I knew Abraham deeply, and he knew Me. A test? Perhaps. But I knew how Abraham would respond."**

"Many believe that Abraham was treated unfairly. The journey to the region of Moriah took three days. Time enough for Abraham to recount over and over again Your words, Your promise, Your covenant. Abraham's trust was complete."

"Abraham did not blindly follow an arbitrary command from an uncaring God. Nor was he being

given a test to prove his love for Me. Our relationship had been established long before. I loved Abraham deeply, and wanted to give him a glimpse of that love. I furthermore wished to share with him the greatest act of love ever recorded in the history of the world. No, this wasn't a test of faith. Abraham was given a vision into the culmination of Our covenant."

"Abraham knew the promised heir would come through Isaac, and he trusted Your command. He figured that You would either stop the sacrifice, or raise Isaac from the dead. Such a sad scene, Father, as he placed the firewood on Isaac's back, and told the two servants to stay with the donkey. When Abraham said that "we" will come back to you…wow! Impenetrable faith! That journey would thrill his heart until the end of his earthly days!"

"My Son, because Abraham and I walked so closely, I trusted him. No test was necessary because I knew the outcome already. I had always known the outcome. That experience was the only way for Abraham to discover how much he trusted Me. Abraham bound his only son and positioned him on the altar, and Isaac went there willingly; just as You, My Son, will do one day. Abraham felt the same sadness all the heavenly hosts will feel in the moments before You are slain. He caught a glimpse of Our love, Our sacrifice. Right then, I stayed Abraham's hand, and renewed the covenant established long before.

"My beautiful Son, I already know everything about My children. These experiences are given for their benefit. Because of Abraham's obedience, his heart was satiated with My love, he was encouraged with the arming of his faith, and he was given a glimpse into My very heart."

PRAYER: Father, may I learn to trust You, just as Abraham did!

Further study: Genesis 15-22

GOD IS MERCIFUL

"*Father, when the children of Israel rebelled at the foot of Mt. Sinai, it appeared that they had caused irreversible damage. Fear entered Moses' heart. It became his darkest moment, darkest because he did not know You well enough to understand what was coming next. You invited him to come into Your presence, and to view the reality of Your character. While on that mountain You proclaimed before him the essence of who You are. You said,* **'The LORD, the LORD God, compassionate and gracious, slow to anger, and abounding in loving kindness and truth; who keeps loving kindness for thousands, who forgives iniquity, transgression and sin; yet He will by no means leave the guilt unpunished, visiting the iniquity of fathers on the children and on the grandchildren to the third and fourth generations.'** *The first part of that verse I fully understand; it is the last part which troubles Me. Help Me to grasp what You mean. Is there a limit to Your mercy?*"

"**A huge misunderstanding must be cleared up, Son. If one is not careful, it would be easy to believe that a child is born with the entire awareness of all that went on before his arrival on this earth. Keep in mind: a baby shows up on this earth, which is not of his choosing, is born into a family not of his choosing, in a condition not of his choosing. This child is absolutely perfect, with all the ability to navigate through this earth. He is priceless. He takes on his belief about himself, his value and his position, from being on this earth. How can I be angry with him?**

How can I blame him for what his parents did?

"Son, here is the problem: I intended the parents should tell their children about Me, if they tell them anything at all; but whatever they tell their children will come from what they have been told, or gathered from their exposure to life. It would seem the children would have no chance at all. I have to start from scratch with everyone who enters this world."

"Father, it appears hopeless. What did You do?"

"I did for them what I did for You. Understand that each child born into this world has the body which has been affected by the deterioration sin caused each preceding generation, and with a nature which is separated from Me. I must reintroduce Myself to each child entering this world, and give him the chance to accept Me, and invite Me into his life. You were born with the body which has been exposed to all those generations of sin, but You were born connected to Me. I invite each human being to know and trust Me by surrounding the child with love from the mother and father. I instructed parents to read to the children from the scriptures. The Spirit of God attends that child throughout his life. The angels of heaven care for him, pointing out the beauties in nature around him, and telling him the stories of what I did in the past. I must give every child a chance to accept Me. The only way is for them to behold My true love for them. The Holy Spirit does all he can to reveal My love in order to prevent them from experiencing the ultimate effects of sin. But, as You have seen, often the child does not have a chance. I try to surround that child with My love, and treat him with kindness, knowing this is the only way to turn the

child to Me. I never use force."

"But what about Korah? The earth opened up and swallowed him and his followers, and all of their families and possessions. That had to have caused fear! Help Me to understand."

"Remember, Son, My children had come from over four hundred years of slavery, from the darkest understanding of what a god is. They were forced to worship creatures and a man. Fear and lies were the primary forces driving religion. For every miracle I performed to deliver them, the father of lies would try to counter all I did in order to cause confusion, murmuring, and insubordination. They were a people in chaos. I worked through Moses to set up order. I gave them symbols to help them understand forgiveness and right doing, and how to connect to Me again. The Liar got some of them to murmur and rebel, and challenge the system and the leaders I appointed.

"Korah, Moses' cousin, the foremost leader of the rebellion, was assigned to tabernacle services. Korah, conceived of a plot to overthrow Moses and Aaron. Joining in the rebellion were Dathan and Abiram, two princes of the tribe of Reuben. Their lies were spreading among the people and a massive unrest was beginning to form in their hearts.

"I performed miracle after miracle to lead My children to trust Me. I gave the children evidence that would lead them to repentance and trust. But they refused every effort of the Holy Spirit. The more Korah did, the harder their hearts became. What more could I do? There was nothing that would change them.

"Moses told the people to move away from the

tents of Korah, Dathan, and Abiram. Then he told the people, 'If those men die of natural cause, then I, Moses, am wrong and Korah should be followed. If they die from an unnatural event, you will know that is from the Lord.'

"I had to withdraw My protection and allow Korah, his family, and his followers to be swallowed up by the earth.

"It was an act of mercy to spare them and those who followed them from destroying themselves. I had to allow the effects of sin take its course by withdrawing My protection. This, Son, is My wrath, merely the removal of My protection."

PRAYER: "Oh, Father, may my heart be open to You, to behold Your love and glory, that I may learn to trust You, and be drawn to You."

Further Study : Numbers 16, 17.

FATHER, WHY ARE YOU SO PATIENT?

"*Father, I have an interesting question this morning.*"
"**What is it Son?**"
"*Going through the scriptures I see so many stories of how men have turned their backs on You: Stories of Cain, tower of Babel, Samson. Jonah ran from You. Over and over Your chosen children Israel rejected You. How could You be so patient with these type of people?*"

"**That is an excellent question, My Son. Let Me try to explain.**

"**First of all, every child on this earth I love with all My heart. Every child on this earth I pursue with My everlasting love. My greatest desire for every one of My children is to have a relationship with Me that will last for eternity.**

"**Sadly, My Son, because My children all have free choice, many of My children turn their backs on Me and reject Me.**"

"*That's my point Father… Why do You go through this pain?*"

"**Jesus, do remember when You were 12 and teaching in the temple? Your parents thought they had lost You. Do You remember when they found you how happy they were? They cried as they hugged You and kissed You.**

"**That is why I am so long-suffering with all My children. When one comes home to Me, I feel the same joy as Your parents did when they found You. I cry and hug and kiss them.**

"**I told Zephaniah that I clap and dance.**

"I go through the suffering just to have the joy when a child returns.

"I told Isaiah that even though a Mother could forget her suckling child, I never could forget My child.

" I even have My children's names engraved on the palms of My hand.

"I long to have, My Son, that joy for every one of My children who chose to have a relationship with Me."

"Father, I understand Your love for every one of Your children, and I will show that love wherever I go. You are a long-suffering God, full of ever-lasting love."

PRAYER: Thank You, Father, for having <u>MY</u> name on the palms of Your hands.

Further study: Jeremiah 13:27, Isaiah 49:15-16, Hosea 11:1-8, Zephaniah chapter 3

GOD WANTS ME
TO BE HIS FRIEND

"*Father, why have You brought Me into Your presence and shown Me the realities of heaven like this? Please don't take Me wrong, I am not ungrateful, this is exactly what I imagined it would be like to be next to You. The world I have come from is so dark; dark in the sense that it is empty of the light I have discovered about You in Scripture and nature, and now, what You have revealed to Me here.*"

"**Son, I have so much I want to share with You. Do You recall what Isaiah said about Your going into the earth and that he referred to it as a place of darkness?**

'The people who walk in darkness will see a great light

Those who live in a dark land, the light will shine on them.

Thou shalt multiply the nation, Thou shalt increase their gladness

They will be glad in Thy presence as with the gladness of harvest,

As men rejoice when they divide the spoil.

For Thou shalt break the yoke of their burden and the staff of their shoulders...

For a child will be born, a son will be given to us;

And the government will rest on His shoulders;

And His name will be called Wonderful, Counselor, Mighty God

Eternal Father, Prince of Peace.

There will be no end to the increase of His government,

Or of peace, on the throne of David and over his kingdom,

To establish it and to uphold it with justice and righteousness

From then or forever more. The zeal of the LORD of Hosts will accomplish this.'

Isaiah 9:2-6

"Oh, My Son, can You see how You are the answer to this scripture, and how You will bring light to dispel the darkness? How You will bring gladness to them forever? For You will tell them that I am for them, and not against them? You have been a bridge builder while on earth, now You will be the bridge builder to span the chasm which has been created by the slanderer, who told lies about Me, and created the gulf between Me and My children. My children have been told I have anger toward them for being born into this world; this has created the gulf.

"Jesus, Your name, Prince of Peace, spells out Your mission; and that is to reconnect heaven and earth. You will reveal to them that from the foundation of the universe I have loved them and have forgiven them; they don't have to work or earn My love. I have set their destiny to be with Us in heaven. Tell them that when Lucifer fell I repeatedly went after him to restore him back to his original position. I was trying to stop the early effect of sin before it seared off his ability to comprehend love, and to have him return; but to no avail.

"This is what they don't understand. Sin does not anger Me toward them, it causes Me to be angry at the

consequences sin has on My children. Sin destroys them and their capacity to grasp Truth. Sin will kill them. **THAT IS WHAT I'M TRYING TO SAVE THEM FROM!** Salvation heals. It restores. It increases the sinners capacity to grasp Truth!

"Remind them, Son, that I had the prophets write out what My heart and mind is like toward them. Lead them to search the scriptures again and again, to see it is I who pursued Adam and Eve when they chose to believe the father of all lies. I restricted Satan to only one place in the entire Garden of Eden and that was the tree of knowledge of good and evil; and then I warned My children to stay away from it. Jesus, how is it that they overlooked the fact that it is I who pursued them in the Garden? It is I who set up the place of worship at the east end of the Garden and stationed My angels and the Shekinah glory, a symbol of My presence, so I could be with them.

"Let them know that I want them to allow Me to be with them in their heart and mind; I want to be their Friend."

"Father, I will point out to them how several of those You were with referred to You as their Friend. Look at Enoch. He walked with You, and You took him right into heaven to remain there for eternity. Then there was Job, who, in his great agony, never blamed You; he felt free to request an audience with You to understand what was happening to him. Abraham and Moses both claimed You as their best Friend. I remember how Moses told the children of Israel there was no need to fear You. Moses knew You so well that he knew You would not abandon them.

"Oh, Father, I pray You will empower Me to tell the glorious good news of Who You really are."

PRAYER: Dear Daddy, open my eyes that I may be able to behold and understand Who You are.

Further Study: Genesis 3,
Genesis 15-22,
Job 15-17

KING HEZEKIAH

God intended to be the Leader of the Children of Israel. When they went through the wilderness in the daytime He was the cloud that gave them air conditioning. At night He was the fire that gave them heat. In the desert He gave them food and water. In those 40 years their clothes were never tattered, their feet were never blistered, and their bodies were fine. God intended to be their Leader, but the children did not want that.

"Tell me, Father, what was their problem? Why were they not satisfied with You, the Giver of all things they needed?"

"They had judges and prophets, but as they looked around them, they noticed that the other nations had kings, and so they wanted a king. I told them that was not a good idea, that the king would want their wealth and their land. But they didn't care. They insisted they wanted a king. And, so, Jesus, since I always meet people where they're at, I told them I would help them find a king. They wanted Saul, and that didn't turn out very well. Then there was David, and Solomon. After Solomon, and up to King Ahaz, there were no good kings. King Ahaz was a terrible king. He led Israel into idolatry. He made the temple into idols. He did everything he could to destroy the Children of Israel. When Hezekiah, the son of King Ahaz, became king, he wanted to turn things around. What would you do, Son, to turn a nation around?"

"I would start taking those idols down. I would build altars to

You. I would clean up the temple. I would make it a place where people could worship You."

"You see, Son, to the Israelites the temple was God, so Hezekiah had to clean it up. He brought the attention of the people back to the temple because that is where they came to meet Me."

"One of the things that Hezekiah did was reinstate Passover. Why was that important?"

"For over 100 years the Israelites did not celebrate Passover. Hezekiah wanted to Children of Israel to remember that they could be delivered from idolatry and their past by observing Passover. Passover was to remind the people that spiritually they were slaves to sin, but I am the One who delivers them from sin. Hezekiah reminded them that I am a God of love, mercy, and deliverance."

"I understand that Hezekiah did well to bring the peoples' attention back to You. But then, in the midst of all the good he was doing, You allowed him to get sick, to suffer. The prophet even visited him and told him he was going to die. What about his sickness, Father? Was that a test to see if Hezekiah would know You better, and understand Your love for him?

"Hezekiah doubted the messenger, Son. He asked for a sign to prove it was MY message that was being delivered. I heard his prayer and told him he was granted 15 more years. I gave him a sign: I set the sundial back 10 degrees. He had an additional 15 years to show My children Who I am. And then…ambassadors from heathen nations hear about what is happening and come to ask a very important question: 'TELL US ABOUT THE GOD YOU SERVE!' Hezekiah answered by showing them all his wealth: gold, silver, statues. And guess what he

doesn't mention? Me and My love for My children. So the ambassadors go back to their countries and talk about the wealth, and then plot to take Judah into captivity.

"I tested Hezekiah so he could see what was in his own heart. The testing was for him, not Me. Hezekiah had one of the greatest opportunities to witness to heathen nations. But somewhere, in that 15 years, he became self-centered, and did not reveal what I am like."

"So, Father, what you are saying is that sometimes you allow circumstances to happen in Your children's lives, not to test them to see if they trust You, but to test their hearts to see how they will handle the circumstances. You allow people to come into Your children's lives so they can show them what You are like."

"Yes. Even though Hezekiah got caught up in his own wealth and success, the one thing for certain is that I always loved him. I always cared for him. I met him where he was. I knew his heart.

We don't know the ending of Hezekiah's story, but we do know that God always loved him!

PRAYER: Lord, send someone into my life that I may show them the glory of Your love.

Further Study: 2 Kings chapters 18-20,
2 Chronicles chapters 29-32

LUCIFER, LIGHT BEARER, TO SATAN, BEARER OF DARKNESS

"*Father, I'm overwhelmed. What I have discovered in Scripture, and found out by Your handiwork in nature, is so vastly different than what I'm hearing from the teachers of religion. They paint a picture of You as One to be feared; that You are arbitrary, severe, and not forgiving. Your kindness overwhelms me! Why did the one who bore the light of our goodness throughout the universe become the bearer of darkness? Every word out of his mouth is a lie. How did that happen?"*

"There is nothing which can justify this condition. What more could I have done? When this universe was created We determined it would be on the basis of love and freedom of choice, not forced obedience. Everyone would act out of the love which was written on each heart. Separating from the Life-Giver is beyond reason."

"*Father, I read the descriptions given by Isaiah and Ezekiel about the fall of Lucifer. They portrayed him as the most beautiful of all Your created beings. He stood nearest to Your throne, observed everything about You, and praised You for Your love and kindness.*"

"It was You he became jealous of. You, too, spread the light of My love. You became one with the angels. They adored You. Trouble was, Lucifer felt he needed to be receiving the same glory as You. He allowed his mind to ignore the fact that You, too, are the Mighty God, the Everlasting Father. Lucifer had

the love and adoration of all the angels. They completely trusted him. Lucifer had to create an illusion to convince the angels he was deserving of spontaneous worship; therefore he invented lying. In all the history of the universe a lie had never been told. Why would those trusting angels doubt his words or motives now? Anything I would have said at that point would have caused complete closure of any openness Lucifer had with Me. I had to find the right moment to appeal to him in love, and to awaken him to the awareness of where his thoughts were leading.

"There was a time when Lucifer grasped what he was doing and was sorrowful to the point of tears. I rejoiced with him. I even danced with delight over his awakening I immediately reinstated him. But My joy was short-lived. Lucifer was amazed at the influence a lie had. He had the angels in the palm of his hand and he could not let go of that exhilaration of creating a false concept and having the angels believe him.

"Some of my precious friends believed his lies and took it upon themselves to convince the doubters to support Lucifer. It was then that there was division among the angels, and a war of ideas began. I called a meeting of all the inhabitants of heaven together and laid out before them who You are, and Your place in the universe. They had never questioned who You are. Up to that point they had no reason to disbelieve Lucifer.

"What more could I have done? It was then that I had to banish Lucifer and his followers from having access to heaven. With just a word I could have caused Lucifer to not exist. I could have wiped any memory of him away from all the angels' minds. But I

had to let the universe see the consequences of sin. Sin, let go, will kill the creature, the creation, and even try to kill the Creator. It was after his exclusion from heaven that We created the earth. We could have told Our children all was a lie. But it is Our word against his. We had to let this controversy play out to the end so all could see without a doubt, what sin does."

"Love was written on the smallest mote of the sunbeam, and on the greatest star in the universe. Adam and Eve were a perfect reflection of Our image. They were even endowed with the ability to create children their own image. Not a blemish was found in them or in all of creation.

"But Son, that dreaded day came. Satan, through the serpent, sowed seeds of distrust of Us in the holy pair. They believed him, and that started the earth on a downward spiral that We had warned about: sin causes death."

"But Father, one mistake, only one sin? Why such a harsh reaction to such a small thing?"

"That's the thing with sin. It's like a leaf on a beautiful plant? Once severed, the source of life cannot complete its flow into the leaf. It cannot be forced to reconnect. It dies."

"So Satan has passed the chance of coming back?"

"The door is always open, but he will not, cannot return. The sinner must choose to come back, and only a revelation of My love will set and keep the sinner free. Every evidence of love I showed Satan, he rejected. Sin does its insidious thing; it changes the person, making it impossible to return. Death is the immediate result. So I had to suspend the natural, immediate result of sin in order to give them another *chance. At this point no one had tasted of the second death. No one, that is, until You.*

"Your mission is to demonstrate Our love to Our children. I will have to stand back and allow You to suffer at the hands of the wicked one and endure the sins of the entire world on Your shoulders. That experience will demonstrate to the entire universe, including unfallen worlds, what the result of sin is.

"Notice what the Devil did. As soon as the holy pair sinned, the Liar screamed out to all the universe: 'NOW WATCH! SEE WHAT THIS LOVING GOD WILL DO!' Much to his shock and embarrassment, We immediately provided the way back. The full display of Our love will be seen through You. All will see the depth to which We will go to save Our children."

Jesus threw Himself into the Father's arms and cried out, *"This is the only way to bring Our children home. I will descend into the depths of hell, and call them home."*

PRAYER: Heavenly Father, thank You that You, Your Son, and the Holy Spirit have pledged to bring me home. You are welcomed into my heart. Keep me through Your love.

Further Study: Genesis 3; 22.
Psalms 22-24.

JOB

"Son, what comes to mind when you hear the name Job? Faith? Patience? Wealth? Definitely Job was an influential presence in his community. He had ten children, and owned seven thousand camels, five hundred yoke of oxen, five hundred donkeys, and servants galore. In ancient times, one would call him blessed. Everything seemed to be going Job's way…until it didn't. I'd like to talk with You about a little wager Satan approached Me with, thinking he could make My good friend Job crumble."**

"Father, I see that Satan appeared in heaven one day and declared that he represented Earth. You asked if he knew Your good servant Job. He answered that Job only served You because he was the richest man in town and that You had bought Job's loyalty. How little Satan understands Your children, Father. Earthly riches can become a burdensome yoke to destroy lives; but not Job's. No matter how much wealth Job gained, he continued to live an upstanding life. Why did you allow this disaster to befall him?"

"Jesus, My children get so enmeshed in their earthly lives. They forget there is a war going on between good and evil and the whole Universe is watching. Satan approached Me with a question, a dare, really: would Job still serve Me if he was stripped of all earthly possessions? I allowed the experiment to begin, but Satan was not to lay a finger on Job. Remember, nothing surprises Me. I knew the outcome, and knew Job's story would bless and

encourage those who go through periods of deep despair."

"Father…all of Job's children, every one, were slain! His animals and servants were stolen or destroyed! Miraculously, Job continued to praise You. But that wasn't the end. Satan covered Job with painful boils from the top of his head to the soles of his feet. Job endured the worst pain Satan could inflict without killing him. In the midst of that humiliation Your good friend remained faithful.

You see, Jesus, trust is a beautiful thing. Because Job trusted Me, nothing could separate him from Me. That is not to say he wasn't suffering. He was so disfigured by the sores that when his three friends came to comfort him, they wept loudly from afar and threw dust on their heads in mourning. Then, they sat with Job in silence for seven days while he contemplated his lot. I was thankful his friends were silent. Good friends, they were.

"At the end of the seven days Job opened up his mouth and cursed his day of birth; but he didn't curse Me, as his wife had strongly suggested. And then his friends began to talk, the first one asking him what he had done wrong, placing the blame for the tragedy directly on Job himself. Oh, it hurts Me when My children think I am punishing them for their behavior. I never do that."

"Father, over and over again I've seen Your hand of love leading, sheltering, blessing, comforting Your children. How could they think You would punish them? If only they could see with Our eyes."

"Yes, Jesus, I know. Job's friends threw in words of disdain and doubt. They accused Job by saying that if he were righteous, this wouldn't have happened; and that Job's questions to Me were going unanswered. Job did begin to question himself, and then he began

talking. But, you know what, Jesus? He was talking to Me! Beautiful words, really. I dearly love to have my children tell Me what is on their minds. I don't care at all if they repeat themselves a hundred times! I just love that they converse with Me. I want them to know that I am their best friend, and best friends talk together! Job was reduced to nothing…no wealth, no family. He was unhappy, and had every right to ask, 'Why?'

"Those friends became toxic to Job when they could have encouraged and supported him in his grief. I wish My children would be more like You, Jesus, when trying to help one another. Eventually, Job realized their words were utterly worthless. He wanted to plead his case before Me, because he was confident in our relationship. Of course I knew that. I'm sure Job's friends thought they were doing the right thing, but when Job realized within himself that he had done nothing wrong, and that our relationship was good, the Universe rejoiced! I wish all My children would be this assured of our relationship, because I am always on their side. ALWAYS."

"Father, Job never did find out why all this happened to him. Can you imagine how thrilled he will be when he hears that You thought enough of him to say to the Universe 'My good friend Job would not let Me down.' What a reckoning! And to know that his wish was granted and his words were inscribed for all to read, for all time!"

"Jesus, Job's words to Me are some of the most beautiful I've ever heard. I just can't wait to see My good friend and rejoice with him. I am so grateful he trusted Me."

PRAYER: Father, It's good to know that we can praise You and we can also share our burdens with You.

Further study: Job 1:1-12 & 20,
Job chapter 8 & 42

ONLY ONE SOLUTION

"Son, from the foundation of the universe, there's been the dilemma We have had to face. And no matter how We looked at the dilemma, there was only one solution.

"We wanted a creation that was a reflection of Who We are. We have such love and respect for one another, and Our love can only be expressed in an environment of complete freedom of choice.

"When We attempt to define what love looks like, We run the risk of being misunderstood. Some will say that I really don't mean it. Others will make a religion out of the definition, and then think this is what they need to do so We accept them."

Frustrated, the Father continues, *"There was never a question by anyone about what principle the universe operated on. People just did right because it was right. Lucifer was the first to question Our love, but not because it was right or wrong. He questioned because You, Jesus, so identified with the angelic world that they adored You.*

"I knew what was in his heart. I tried to help him realize where he was headed. I finally convinced him. He came back, but then his pride would not let him stay. He swayed a third of the heavenly host to believe I had a wicked, selfish, motive. He could find no more sympathetic listeners so he came to this earth.

"Here is the other part of the dilemma. I could not allow the natural consequence of separating from

the Life-giver to occur. The angels would have cut themselves off from life, and cease to exist. I could not let this happen; all the remainder of the angels would not understand. They needed to see that sin results in death, not that I killed them. I could not use force, for this would create more devils.

"By not allowing the full results to happen, I again took a risk. They could conclude they would not die. And they could believe the only solution to sin was for Me to get angry and destroy them, or try to agree with Lucifer, change the law, and acknowledge him as a co-ruler.

"Look at the results. Lucifer convinced Adam and Eve. They distrusted and lost Eden, lost their garment of light, and lost the power to obey and resist the evil one.

"Satan convinced all but a few with his lies and the world headed to total disaster, and ended in a flood. I had to let My children see the results of sin, and to see that only by re-connecting to Me could they resist the devil and become restored to the original design I intended for all humanity.

"The greatest test the unfallen world faced was what happened to the little girl in Judges who was raped and beaten all night. They wanted Me so badly to save her, and pour out fire from heaven to destroy those wicked men. I took a great risk, I said 'No'. I had to let her die. It was the only way I could awaken Israel to see how far they had fallen.

"That little girl will be one of the brightest jewels in heaven. I will honor her. But, Jesus, the greatest trial for them and You is just ahead.

Your life on earth will be a demonstration of what

My mind and heart is like; that I am FOR them and not against them. Your life will also be a demonstration of how horrible sin is. The most religious people on earth who follow all the rules, but don't know Me, will kill their Creator!

"The greatest trial for the angels will be that they will want to destroy those wicked men who torture You. I must say, 'NO!'

"The world must see what love looks like. They must know My heart. And the world must see what sin will do. They then have a choice to make.

"Jesus, You are the only solution! Only You truly know Me. Only You can not sin your entire life. Only You can suffer for all of the world's sins. And only You can come back from the dead. Only You, the Creator God, can offer that victory to all men, and give them a new heart and new mind, and make them and the whole universe safe throughout eternity."

PRAYER: Father, thank You for taking that risk for me and all mankind. Please perform Your work in me, to form me into the likeness of Your precious Son.

Further study: Romans 1-4

THE TOWER OF BABEL

"*Father, after the flood, You established an eternal covenant with Noah, to assure him, and all who came after, that flood waters would "never again" destroy the earth. 'Never' sounds pretty final. What a kind gesture and true blessing this was for Noah and his family, and generations to come! As the earth's surface renewed, earth's population grew as You had commanded. Around the dinner table, at worship, even out in the fields, I can imagine the flood story being told, and retold. Over time, however, the people lost interest in You. Falling away from You, it would only be human, wouldn't it, to wonder if You might destroy the earth again? So the people devised a plan to save themselves. Father, I understand You gave a glorious promise to Your children, that they might live in safety and without fear. What happened? Why were they afraid?*"

"Oh, My Son, My beloved people began to murmur about building a grand city, with a tower going up into the heavens. Not only would it be a monument to their greatness, but a tower in which they would find safety. Of course, I wanted them to run to Me. I longed to be their 'Strong Tower'.

"So, I came down from the heavens to be with My people and see what was going on. You know, I just couldn't stay so far away. I never can when My children have need of Me. I came down to be in their midst, and soon discovered that, indeed, there was to be a tower, built by the people's very own hands."

"*Father, Your reassurance was evidenced in every story passed down from parent to child, in every flower that bloomed, in every star that lit the evening sky And, surely, when they saw the beautiful rainbow.*

"I cannot understand putting faith and trust in a structure built of mud and tar when the very heavens declared Your glory. I think of the unimaginable labor needed to build a tower reaching into the heavens. What a waste of time when the people already had everything they needed. But perhaps they weren't placing faith in a building. Perhaps their mistake was placing faith in themselves. There must be more to this story."

"When man separates himself from Me, he comes up with all kinds of crazy ideas. Surely, this was one, and I couldn't let it happen. Plans apart from Me always fail for eternity. If the people were successful, nothing would stop them in their prideful quest to be self-sufficient, to rule the world. So I did the improbable. I confused their languages, and that made working together impossible. As those with one language found one other, they regrouped and scattered apart from the others. How many languages I created in that single moment, I couldn't even tell You. But it was enough."

"So with the confused languages, the efficient workers were stopped in their tracks! The sudden crisis of communication created a quandary of confusion and, like ants, people immediately swirled in a multitude of directions…exactly the result You needed. So when the construction on the Tower of Babel, which means "confusion", ended right then and there, the people were scattered far and wide."

"My Son, I came down into the world when mankind had forgotten about Me. My children were moving in a path of sure destruction. My love demands that I do everything within My power to save them from the lust of the world. Just as You, Jesus, have come into the world at its darkest hour to offer

hope and salvation to all who will believe in Me."

PRAYER: Thank you, Father, for caring enough to intercede in the lives of Your children. Thank you for being my 'Tower of Safety'.

Further Study: Genesis 9:11,
Proverbs 18:10

LOT

Some who study the Sodom and Gomorrah story wonder if Lot was worth saving: others wonder how God could destroy the inhabitants of two cities, how God could turn Lot's wife into a pillar of salt, and how Lot could offer up his two daughters. But, in keeping with God's character, how might one explain this unsettling event in earth's history? What do the facts show?

Both abundantly blessed, Abram's and Lot's rich possessions were stretching thin the resources of the land. The herders had begun to complain, and the disturbance trickled up to their employers. Seeking peace between the families, Abram suggested they move and He gave Lot "first choice" on the land. Lot made a whole string of bad choices from the time he "cast his lot" with Uncle Abram, until his wavering exit from Sodom. This was one of them.

"Father," said Jesus, "culture would have demanded that Abram decide, but he was willing to take left-overs. Why?"

"My dear Son, when children put their trust in Me, they make kingdom choices. Abram and I were friends, and I had blessed him. We talked frequently. When You make kingdom choices, You don't worry about having more, or less. You consider the other's best. Abram magnanimously offered Lot the best that he could envision. Without deferring to Abram's seniority, Lot looked at the lush vegetation and gardens surrounding the big city of Sodom, and grabbed it. I was sad Lot made that choice, for I knew well the city and its inhabitants. Hardships would

come, including war, with Lot and his family taken as prisoners. But, even after the daring rescue by Uncle Abram, Lot chose to go right back. I wish he had talked with Me first."

In ensuing years, God made a covenant with Abram, and changed his name to Abraham, father of many. One afternoon, Abraham was out in the heat of the day and saw three men approaching his tent. He hurriedly selected a tender calf and saw to the visitors' needs. Soon, Abraham realized he was speaking with two angels, and God Himself…

"Jesus, news of the wickedness of Sodom and Gomorrah had reached Me, and I wanted to see for Myself what was going on. So, I came down to talk with my friend, Abraham. While there, I reminded him of our covenant; and then, Jesus, I wanted to include him in My plans. I long for conversation with My children and want them to share what's on their minds. As I suspected, Abraham protested, 'Lord, if there are 50 righteous?' I told him the people of Sodom and Gomorrah had openly rejected Me; that they took great pride in their gardens, and vegetation, and sexual pleasures…and had need of nothing. 'But Lord, if there are 45,' He pleaded; if there are 40? 30? 20? 10?' Jesus, I told Abraham that if there were ten righteous, the cities would be spared. Absolutely!"

"Again, Father, You must have known there were not ten righteous people in these cities. Even Lot's own family laughed at the warnings."

"Yes, I knew the people were so dark in sin that they would not listen, but I had promised Abraham, and I keep My promises. I sent two more angels down to earth, right to the city gate where Lot sat. He

invited them to his home. During the course of the evening, all the men of the city formed outside, pounding on the door and demanding the two visitors. Lot offered them his daughters."

"Why would Lot offer his daughters to this mob of angry men?" asked Jesus.

"Just the question so many have asked. Lot was familiar with the depths of deprivation in this city. He counted on the fact that they weren't interested in women, but he wasn't prepared when they came after him! The Angels grasped Lot, pulled him into the house, and blinded the mob. You would think the sudden blindness would get the attention of everyone. Sadly, no one even asked Me about it; and when the two angels warned Lot to collect his family because I was about to destroy the city, he hesitated. When he hesitated, the men grasped his hands and the hands of his wife and of his two daughters and led them safely out of the city, for I was merciful to them.

"Jesus, I don't know what else I could have done at that point, but I wasn't through. In Your ministry, meet people where they are...doubt, despondency, despair, disease...and do everything You can to save them. Much of the time, it takes great patience. Lot and his wife had a beautiful home filled with lovely possessions. Family members wouldn't join them. Because of this, I knew they would be pulled back into the city if they lingered and looked back. I pled with them NOT to look back, to keep running to the mountains. Two things happened. Lot thought he would rather go to the city of Zoar, so I patiently assured him I would not destroy the city; and Lot's wife turned back. If she returned, her family would

surely follow. Perhaps turning her into a pillar of salt seems cruel, but her fate would have been far worse had she returned."

"Father, Your agreement was for ten, and there were only three. How gracious You are! But when Lot changed his mind again and went to live in the mountains, why didn't You give up?"

"Son, these were the best three out of the entire city, and I moved heaven and earth to save them. How can I do less for My children? I blessed Lot abundantly, delivered him from capture, blinded the angry mob, saved him from the destruction of Sodom; and yet he never could trust Me completely. In the end his daughters each had a son by their father, and these two nations became some of the worst enemies of Israel. I wanted so much more for these three."

"No one can doubt Your great love for mankind, Father. But, when man turns away from You, the evidence of Your love cannot be seen, nor understood. You must have wept as You watched those magnificent cities destroyed by fire."

"Jesus, it doesn't matter how many times man fails. The second he turns to Me, I am there. In fact, I am always available to converse, to encourage, to provide…even to weep. Yes, I wept for the people of Sodom and Gomorrah, just as I do for all who turn away from Me."

PRAYER: "Thank you, Father, for grabbing my hand and not letting go."

Further study: Genesis chapters 18&19

THE UNFORGOTTEN CHILD

"Daddy", Jesus began cautiously, *"I can't keep back a question which has been bothering Me much of My life. I don't mean to question Your wisdom, or plans. I also know I can't hide My thoughts from You, so I'm going to voice it. Why Judges? Why did You allow it to be placed in Your sacred scroll?"*

"Jesus", His Father responded, **"remember David's Psalms which states, 'Even though My child walks in the valley of the shadow of death, I will be with him.' Well, I had to reveal the measureless depth to which man can sink when he has thrown aside My word, and I still will rescue him.**

"Another major reason is that, when man has no guidance, he is like a rudderless ship in a strong storm. He can't find a safe harbor, and he leaves in his wake many innocent victims. My promises are for those often forgotten, tortured souls. I don't want them to think I have forgotten them!

"Let Me explain about one of My most precious treasures who was one of those victims, and in the process give You the bigger picture.

"First, realize nearly one quarter of the book of Judges is dedicated to this child. I don't want anyone to think she passed by unnoticed.

"Second, remember, two times I had emphatically had said the children of Israel forgot Me. They did what was right in their own eyes."

Jesus interjected, *"Oh yes. I remember and I know well the story. A man who was a priest traveling with his concubine tried to find a safe place to stay for the night and he picked a 'god-fearing town.'"*

Disgusted at the thought, Jesus cringed and said, *"This worthless fellow was instructed to stay with one of the good men in the town. Those wicked men of that city wanted to abuse the priest. But instead, the man of the house and the priest gave those disgusting citizens his concubine!"* In disbelief, Jesus added, *"After all night of abuse, she died at the front step of the house. That heartless priest gets up in the morning, opens the door, says to her, 'come on, get up, lets go.'"*

Jesus could hardly get the rest of the story out. *"He discovered she had died. He packs her home on a donkey, chops her up in twelve pieces, send messengers with the pieces to the twelve tribes."* Jesus, with tears streaming down His cheeks, cries out, *"How can they get so low?"*

His Daddy tightly embraced His Son to comfort Him, and said, **"Let Me show You the bigger picture. When the tribes received those body parts, it shocked them into reality of how far they had fallen, and they slayed those miserable, wicked men.**

"But here is the bigger picture: all heaven witnessed it. They wanted to rescue her, I had to restrain them. They had to grasp the horrible, ugly depths that separation from Me will take a person. This was hard for the angels to understand.

"Let Me add the deeper reason." His Daddy held His Son at arm's length, looked into His eyes and said, **"that little girl, unknowingly, prepared the universe for what will happen to You."**

"How?" Jesus asked.

"These godless, empty priests You will be witnessing to about My love for them, will ignore all

You have said, and abuse You beyond belief," the Father added with tears flowing down His face. *"Once again the heavenly host will want to rescue You; but I will have to restrain them. They have to see that what I said in the beginning is true: Sin, or separation from Me, will kill victims, will kill the sinner, and will even kill God!*

"You see, that little child helped the entire universe be prepared to see not only how far sin will go, but also that You are willing to suffer the full extent of sin for all men, so they don't have to. The people will also see that You conquered sin and death, and silenced the accusations and lies the Devil has said about Us. You will come forth from that grave and offer Your victory and new life to all who accept You!

"That, My Son, is the whole story of My precious treasure soon to be honored to the height of heaven because of the gift of her life," the Father said, beaming with joy.

PRAYER: Thank You Father for giving us the bigger picture. Like Paul, I agree; may You show Yourself mighty as You present Your case in the courts of the universe. May I be an example of Your promise, "All those who labor and are heavily burdened come unto Me. I will put my law within you, and fashion you into the image of Your Son."

Further study: Romans 8-12

JONAH

"*Father, why did You chose to send Jonah to Ninevah? Why?*"

"Ninevah was the largest city and known for its wickedness and the center of crime. The people had no regard for human life. But, they were still My children and I loved them. I wanted Jonah to bring a message of repentance to Ninevah and to tell them they had 40 days to turn their lives around. I told Jonah exactly what to do. You can imagine what the adversary told Jonah: 'Why would you want to do this? The people are probably not going to listen to you, they might even kill you.' Even though I spoke directly to Jonah, he became discouraged. He forgot I am all-wise and all-powerful."

"*But Father, Jonah blatantly disobeyed You and went in the opposite direction from Ninevah.*"

"Yes, I was working with Jonah. I was not going to give up on my friend. I wanted to get his attention to let him know that I still cared. Jonah had made up his mind, and in his mind he thought he made the right decision. So I sent a great wind, the sea got rough, and the sailors began to pray to their gods, but nothing got any better. Finally one of the sailors remembered Jonah and woke him up, and told him to pray to his God. Jonah realized he was the problem because he was not following what I had told him to do. His solution was to have the sailors throw him overboard. As soon as they threw him overboard, I *stopped the winds and calmed the sea."*

"Father, after Jonah was thrown into the sea You sent a great fish. Why the great fish?"

"My Son, you can imagine what went though Jonah's mind as he reflected on his life while he was in the great fish. That is exactly what I wanted him to do. Jonah called upon Me to remember him. I could never forget him. That's all I wanted – Jonah to trust Me. I listened to his prayer and then had the great fish spit him out on land. After I got his attention, I again told him that I wanted him to go to Ninevah. Jonah went and the people repented and said they would listen to Me. Even the King of Ninevah made a proclamation for everyone to turn from their evil ways. I sent Jonah to that wicked city because the people there are My children. I loved them and wanted a relationship with them. My children turned back to Me. That's what I wanted!"

"But, Father, after the people repented, Jonah got angry because You did not destroy the city. He seemed concerned that the people would think he was a false prophet. He did not remember that you are merciful and compassionate, slow to get angry with even the worst people on earth. He knew You were too good to destroy the city.

"I wanted to save thousands of the worst people. They were My children. I was patient with Jonah even though he tried to run from Me. He was My child. I loved him."

"Father, I can see your patience with Jonah and also with Ninevah. You are so compassionate and so merciful. No one can outrun Your love!"

PRAYER: My Father, it's so reassuring to know that we can never outrun Your love. Thank You for loving me.

Further Study: Jonah's Prayer: Jonah 2:1-9.

NEBUCHADNEZZAR

*"**G**ood morning, My Son.   What would You like to discuss this morning?"*

"Father, I am impressed with Your dealing with King Nebuchadnezzar."

"I'll tell You why I did what I did, My Son.   The kingdom of Babylon were My children also.   Israel would not listen to Me and were wandering away from Me.   I was saddened and had to get their attention.   I sent Isaiah and other prophets to warn them that disaster was coming.   They would not listen! Finally, I removed My protection and they went into slavery in Babylon.   I did not leave them without hope.   I told them slavery would be over in 70 years.   For 70 years My wayward children could witness to Babylon.

"I gave a dream to Nebuchadnezzar that only Daniel could tell him the dream and its interpretation. This accomplished exactly what I wanted. Nebuchadnezzar recognized that there was a God superior to his gods, and he proclaimed this throughout Babylon.

"But he soon forgot Me and decided that he would build an image of gold that everyone would worship.   I had three of My children who would not worship that idol.   King Nebuchadnezzar was angry and cast My friends into a fiery furnace.   I loved King Nebuchadnezzar and so I kept My friends from burning up. King Nebuchadnezzar again realized that there was a God more powerful and loving.   He

proclaimed throughout the nation Who this God was."

"Father, like most of Your children, he still rebelled."

"Yes, My Son, so sad. I gave King Nebuchadnezzar another dream warning him that his ways would lead to his destruction. He would not listen! He really got caught up on himself, lost his mind and ate grass like an animal for 7 years. You know Jesus, after these horrible 7 years Nebuchadnezzar came to his senses. You know what he did? Hhe proclaimed My name throughout the Kingdom. Another child who came home!

"Father, I want to share Your love to every person I can. I want to show them how precious they are to You!"

PRAYER: Father, I realize how precious I am to You. I know You will never give up on me and, Father, I will not give up on You.

Further study: Daniel 2,3 & 4

NEHEMIAH

"*Father, I want to share with you the amazing picture of You that I have discovered. It was the speech that Nehemiah gave to the people who were restoring the walls.*"

"Please share with Me, My Son, your thoughts."

"*Nehemiah recounted how You brought Your children out of bondage from Egypt. You lead them through the Red Sea. You fed them every day with manna. You brought forth water from rocks. You gave cooling in the day with clouds, and warmth with fire at night. You even brought them to the mountain to reveal Your glory and love... They were only 11 days away from the land You had promised them.*

"*I would have thought, Father, they would have been grateful, but they were not. That's unbelievable!! They hardened their hearts against You. They consistently complained, even saying they would be better off in Egypt. They even built a golden calf to worship, not worshiping You, but a golden calf!*

"*Nehemiah pointed out that You did not give up on them. You still fed them, You still provided for them and most of all You still loved them.*

"*The children of Israel eventually got to the promised land. They prospered, but then decided they wanted to be like other nations and be ruled by a King. You shared with them that it was not a good idea, but they wouldn't listen. Again, Your graciousness was shown. You didn't get angry with them. You, instead, helped them find King Saul.*

"*Over and over Your children rebelled against You. They would not listen to Your prophets. They even killed your prophets. Father,*

You always showed them mercy, lovingkindness and compassion.
    "You never gave up on them, but sadly, they gave up on You!
    "Nehemiah was talking to people who had lost everything, who had been in slavery for 70 years, and who came home to rebuild. He reminds them, Father, that You are a God who is just, slow to anger, who shows mercy, never leaves us, and most of all Who loves us."
    "My Son, that is Who I Am!"
    "Father, give Me the strength to show every one who You are."

PRAYER: I am not always grateful, but I know that You love me. I know You will pick me up when I fall.

Further study: Nehemiah chapter 9 (one of the best unknown chapters in the Bible)

WHAT IS MY MISSION?

"Father, what do You want Me to accomplish in My ministry? What do you want Me to do for my fellow man?"

"You know, Jesus, My children do everything right as far as their belief system. They keep the right day for Sabbath. They pay the right amount of tithe. They eat the right food. They have their temple. They have their sacrifice system. They feel very confident in how religious they are. But they have no idea Who I am! They have no idea of how much I love them and how much I care for them. In Your ministry, the thing I would like for You to do the most is to show them a picture of Who I am; show by Your life, by Your actions, by Your beliefs, by Your preaching.

"I have worked hard with My children to lead them to a life where we could have a relationship and they would love Me. I have taken some drastic steps to help that relationship. In the wilderness the people came to Moses and said, 'Moses, we don't want to talk to God anymore. We want to talk to you.' I didn't want that for My children so I instructed Moses to build a sanctuary right in the center of their camp so I could live with them. Throughout the centuries they've taken that very concept of Me being among My people and almost made IT their idol. They love the temple, but they love the services more than they love Me.

"When Adam and Eve decided to wander away

from me, the Life-Giver, I had to get across to them that without Me in their lives, there would be certain death. I had a very simple sacrificial system to demonstrate to them what death was like, and they took that system throughout the centuries and almost made it their right of salvation.. They even perverted the system. Instead of taking the best of the lambs, the best of the cattle, the best of the turtle doves, they picked the sick ones, the lame ones, the unfit ones. My children even took advantage of the poor people by overcharging them for the animals for their sacrifices. They took what I thought would be a meaningful symbolism to them, and again made it their means of salvation. They really don't know Who I am. And, You, My Son, must demonstrate what their Father is like.

"This is not a new problem. I think of Hosea who I sent with a warning to the Children of Israel. Again, they brought up about sacrifices and I had to tell them I would rather have mercy than have their sacrifices. I would rather that they know Who I am and have a knowledge of Me. I want You, Jesus, to paint a picture of Who I really am.

"I had a prophet named Micah, who I sent to Judah and Israel to give a warning. Micah asked Me, 'God, what do You really want from us? Do You want us to bring our burnt offerings. Do You want us to bring oil?' Micah was frustrated and asked, 'Lord, do You want us to bring our firstborn? What do You want from us, Lord?'

"And You know, Jesus, the answer is simple. I want my children to be just. I want them to show mercy. I want them to walk with Me.

"What I want from You, Son, is to be a blessing to everyone. I want You to show the people what I want to do for them. I don't want token sacrifices. I don't want token worship. I don't want token love. I want their hearts. I want relationship. I want to hold them in My arms. I want My children to sit on my lap. I want to go with them throughout their lives.

"As you go about, I want you to show justice to the oppressed. I want you to show them that I care; that when they're seeking hope, it's found in Me and My love. I want You to show people mercy. I want You to demonstrate by Your life what it means to walk humbly with Me.

"As My children walk along the path of life, they are going to stumble. They are going to fall. I want you to show them by Your actions that I am not going to condemn them. I'm not going to leave them. That no matter what they do, I'll pick them up and continue to walk with them. I want them to realize that I am their Friend, that I love them, and I long for us to have discussions, to share our thoughts. As they get to know Me, they will see how much I love them and they will respond to that love.

"I don't want My children to obey Me out of obligation, but in our relationship as we get to know each other, they will want to do the right thing and we will embrace each other.

"I want You to remind them, as I did David, though they walk through the valley of death, I'm there. I want the lepers to know that I care. And I want You to bring healing to them.

"The greatest thing You can do, My Son, is to share with My children that if they have seen You,

they have seen the Father. You are My Son, the reflection of the sun that will bring hope into their lives. So share with the people that I want them to love each other, to treat each other with justice and mercy. Tell them I just want to put My arms around them and walk down the path and journey together.

PRAYER: Father, let me show justice; let me show mercy. Thank you that I can walk side by side with You.

Further study:
Philippians 4,
Galatians 4,5

NOAH

"*Father, were You angry when You decided to allow flood waters to encompass the earth, destroying all that You had lovingly created with Your own hands…every tree, every bird, and every mother and father save one family? I wonder how You could destroy innocent babies in such a horrific and catastrophic event?*"

"Son, about 1500 years after Adam, the earth was filled with powerful and highly intellectual people, beautiful physical specimens of My creative power. The Garden of Eden remained in plain sight, cherubim guarding the entrance. I thought perhaps the flashing sword would remind people of the price of sin; but mankind wandered far from Me, and worshipped the very Nature I created. Their hearts were evil, and their thoughts and actions caused Me to repent having created them. There was only one thing I could do, and my heart ached.

"There was one man who trusted Me. He wasn't perfect, but I never care about that. Trust was important, though, for this man would have to endure ridicule, exhaustion, and doubt for the 120 years' duration of the ark construction. Having ample time to plead for the hearts of My beloved people was so very important to Me. And remember, Jesus, rain was a phenomenon. This man must preach My words without fully understanding the very message he was speaking. Because of our relationship, I trusted Noah."

"I can see the sadness in Your eyes because You hated losing even one of Your children. So, Father, when the ark was completed, and the animals began their orderly march just as You had commanded them to do, why didn't the people respond?"

"Well, Son, one would think My big appeal would surely get their attention. I thought long and hard on how to choreograph the compelling scene. Animals appeared from nowhere and marched right through the door of the ark where Noah and his family waited; every kind, two-by-two. Wouldn't You think that humans who worshipped nature would have been impressed? My ways are love, and I boldly approached the logic of their beliefs. If they witnessed a panoramic viewing of the fulfilling of Noah's 120 year message, and the seeming obedience of nature to My unseen hand, would their hearts turn towards Me? The answer is no: for when mankind separates from Me, sin has no logic."

"I can imagine the mysterious scene unfolding, beginning with Noah and his family entering and exiting the ark to store the massive quantities of food required for all on this journey, all the while continuing to preach the message that held so much promise. I can imagine seeing the parade of animals walking step-in-step with no seeming intent to harm one another. There must have been absolute quiet as the eyes of those gathered were suddenly drawn to the vast wooden door that had allowed the passing of giraffes and elephants tigers, lions, and every slithering creature, slowly swinging shut as if by invisible hand. And then all was still, but Father, for seven days nothing happened. Why did You make Noah wait seven days?"

"I know it was hard on Noah to wait, but the people had now seen several rather startling events. They must have time to ponder, analyze, and hopefully rethink their decision. My heart was still

pleading with them to enter the ark and be saved. Please understand, Jesus, that I roam the earth with one goal in mind, to save mankind from sure destruction. If even one had pounded on the door and sought safety, that door would have been flung open wide to receive him or her. A God of love can only respond with love. If someone had knocked on the door of the ark and asked to be saved, I would say 'Come on in!'"

"I understand. You will do anything to draw Your children to You. Mankind was wicked and had chosen long ago to exclude You. Nothing would cause them to change their decision. Even so, You, Father, being merciful, waited: and then the rain began to fall."

"Can You imagine Lucifer, and the story he would tell to the universe: 'See, I told you that God doesn't care about you!' But I do care for each one and I had to wipe out evil in order to preserve a group that would be faithful, a group that would trust Me; because down the road a Redeemer, You, My Son, would come to bring salvation to all who would call on My name.

"The natural consequences of sin are incredibly hard, Jesus. I may as well tell you now that when mankind experiences unnecessary pain, You will suffer along with each one."

"I understand. My heart is filled with sadness, but because of My relationship with You and My trust in You, I know that the children are in Your hands."

"You, My Son, are the Ark of Safety."

God used an ark and a man to build it. The ark was lifted up where everyone could see it. Whoever walked into Noah's ark found life. Thousands of years later, Jesus Christ was lifted up, and all who look and enter into a relationship with Christ will find life.

PRAYER: Thank you, Father, for providing an ark, so that I can have eternal life.

Further Study: Genesis 6-9

RAHAB

Do You scratch your head when reading about the mighty warriors of faith and you come to the name "Rahab"? For example, we think of Noah, Moses, and Abraham as great men. Oh, they made some tall blunders; but their historical stories are abundant with evidences of faith, obedience, repentance, and leadership. What kind of God would honor Rahab, a prostitute? Well, let's see what God Himself might have told Jesus about this extraordinary woman who knew very little about Him, only what she had gleaned through community gossip.

"Father, I would like to talk about the experience of Rahab."

"Son, I directed Joshua to send two men into the Promised Land to scout it out, and to pay close attention to Jericho. It was there they ran into Rahab, who took them in. That was particularly brave, as she had heard the stories about what I had been doing in the land. Her own people lived in fear that I would conquer Jericho next."

"Father, I love this story because Rahab, shunned by the village and society, was chosen to share an integral part in Your story to the world because You knew her heart. By the way, You sure do have an eclectic circle of friends, Father."

"Yes, I do. Rahab and I had been working on our relationship for a good while. She was a wise woman who listened to truth. Also, she was very loving, and made a bargain with the spies to hide them if they would promise to save not only her, but her mother and father, brothers and sisters...the whole

family…when the army came to conquer Jericho. I was very touched that Rahab was not only concerned with herself, but with her family as well.

"Soon, the king discovered that there were two spies in Jericho and sent men to search for them, eventually coming to Rahab's house. She had hidden them up in the rooftop, but told the men that they had come and left. She lied. I really kind of winced at that because I certainly would have protected the spies, but Rahab was doing what she thought was right. Her bravery was now apparent to all, for not many could have stood up to the king's men. I might have had a little part in that, Jesus. When it was time for the spies to be rescued, Rahab let down a scarlet rope and the spies scrambled down that rope to safety. Conveniently, her house was part of the city wall with just the most perfect window. I do plan things well, Jesus! The spies told the story to Joshua and when Jericho fell, Rahab and her whole family were taken outside the city and saved."

"Father, the life of Rahab gives mankind hope, doesn't it? Though she was a prostitute, not what You had ordained for her life, and though man had written her off…she still found You."

"Oh, Jesus, I loved My daughter Rahab! I wanted so much for her and knew the future she could have if she turned to Me. Mankind sometimes counts as worthless those who don't follow earthly guidelines of success. These people are ridiculed, rejected, and yes, 'written off'. I never quit searching for those who are lost. Never! I was so touched by the fact that, though Rahab had little knowledge of Me, she recognized I was special. She believed the stories of how I led My children through the Red Sea and out of Egypt, and

*how **I** destroyed the two **Amorite kings**. That spark of faith saved her life."*

"Of course, Jesus, one of Rahab's descendants was King David. Also, Rahab is one of your ancestors because the lineage of David came through her. Do you understand now, why I don't focus on words like prostitute? Nothing, absolutely nothing, can deter Me from wanting a relationship with My children; and when they are redeemed, there is simply no limit to what they can achieve through Me."

"Yes, Father. If I ever come across a prostitute, I will remember Rahab and her experience."

PRAYER: Father, thank You for seeing the scarlet rope in my life and rescuing Me.

Further Study: Joshua 2, 6:22-25,
Mathew 15,
John 8

WHY THE LAMB?

The Father and Son were basking in One another's presence. What a picture of serenity- the Daddy enfolding the Son in His arms. In the mind of Jesus there was the thought of how dark was the world He had been in, how hostile and rebellious were the people, how unwelcomed He had felt in the places of worship. Yet, here in the presence of His Father, in the warmth of His embrace, how bright and pure and comforting it was. Jesus noticed how every being of heaven felt safe and happy in His presence; even the smallest of creatures reveled in the safety of His love. Finally, the Father extended His arms, put His hands under the chin of the Son, looked deeply into His eyes and spoke, ***"What is it, My Son? Something is troubling You."***

"Father, I have noticed several things which I cannot understand. The lamb, Father. There are numerous places in the stories which focus on the lamb. As soon as Adam and Eve chose not to believe You, but embraced the lie of the serpent, You rushed them out of the garden. There was a lamb slain. Why?

"Then there was the event with Cain and Abel. Able was approved by You and His sacrifice of the lamb accepted; but Cain's offering of the fruits of his garden were rejected. And Cain slew Able, all over the lamb. Why?

"Then there was the event with Abraham and his son, Isaac. Again there was a lamb. What about the sanctuary in the wilderness? The focus was on those who sinned who brought a lamb for a sacrifice, and then went back to their tents, forgiven. I noticed the priest took the blood of that lamb and sprinkled it in various

places within the sanctuary, especially on the curtain that separated the holy from the most holy place. Why, Father?

"And the most troubling of all was what I read about the Messiah who was often connected with the lamb. There are scriptures describing the Messiah as powerful and glorious, but coupled with that He is portrayed as suffering greatly. Why?"

"My Son, you are the One who has been by my side from times eternal. You spoke and the worlds came into being. You shared My glory and splendor. But before all this happened, You, the Holy Spirit, and I laid down the principles governing the entire universe: all beings will live free; no force will ever be used to govern Our children; the universe would operate on laws of natural results.

"But discord began in the mind of Lucifer. He felt he should get the adoration equal with You, in fact, above You. We entreated him to turn from the path he was taking. He began to spread lies about Us. He said We were liars: arbitrary, vengeful, unforgiving and cruel. We could not allow him to suffer results of his rebellion and die. We let the full results of his thinking play out before the universe. We would not use force.

"After this We created the earth. We had to demonstrate what love could do. We made beings in Our image. Everything was perfect! In the Garden of Eden was the Tree of Knowledge of Good and Evil, the only place on earth at which Satan was allowed to present his case. One day Eve found herself there. The Devil disguised himself as one of the most attractive creatures and convinced Eve to mistrust Us. She partook of the fruit which symbolized partaking of lies. She convinced Adam to take it also. The pair

sensed a darkness and coldness settle down on the earth; their beautiful robes of light were gone. They found themselves naked and ashamed.

"We put into action the plan We laid down from the foundation of the world. We grabbed their hands and ran with them out of the Garden. Then we placed two angels to share the real truth about Us, and to keep the way open to life eternal.

"But words can be cheap and meaningless. A living example had to be provided by living out Our true character, and proving Satan's lies to be wrong. If we went to Our children, they could not stand the glory of our presence.

"But here is the reality of sin: sin, let go, will kill the sinner, kill the creation, and if possible, kill the Creator. The grim reality is that many will not believe, and they will kill the messenger. One must go, and not use any force, to live Our principle of love, and show that God does not kill the sinners. God actually pursues them and tries to keep them from destroying themselves.

"I would go, but the greatest evidence of love is that a Father who loves His Son, would allow Him to demonstrate love and suffer the results of the sinner. That is the greatest sacrifice One can give.

"YOU, MY SON, ARE THAT LAMB!"

PRAYER: Oh, Father, pass the goodness of Your character of love before me. Help me to see the depth of that love that I might not separate from You.

Further study: Isaiah 53

MANASSEH

One of the worst people ever to walk the face of the earth was King Manasseh. The Bible says that he did more evil than the nations God had conquered through Israel and Judah. Can a leopard change spots? We shall see; but, I would encourage you never to give up on God, for He is Elohim, and He will never give up on you.

"Father, You seemed to love meeting with Your children face-to-face, or through a cloud or burning bush. Why, then, did you decide to install kings and judges?"

"My Son, the people had stopped listening to Me, so I built a sanctuary to dwell in their midst. That is where I long to be. But then, yes, they wanted a king so they could be like everyone else. I told them this was not a good idea; but they were persistent, and I offered to help find a king. Some of the kings were very good, and My people prospered. Some were not. King Manasseh was one of the most evil. Even I was not prepared for the evil done under his rule."

"The temple was destroyed to again become a place of idol worship. Children were sacrificed, and Your people were persecuted. Father, What was to be gained from his reign?"

"Jesus, it is difficult to watch such destruction, but I cannot choose for My children the path they take. I work with what is given to Me. King Hezekiah, Manasseh's father, listened to Me and was a good king. He restored the temple and its system so beautifully, brought water into Jerusalem and

repented of his wrong. Hezekiah enjoyed great wealth and honor, and left a legacy of prosperity. Why, I even granted him 15 more years of life, as You know. Things couldn't have turned out more differently for his son.

"I always prepare My children for what is going to happen. To Manasseh, I sent the prophet Isaiah, and the message was not good. Disaster would come to Jerusalem and Judah, disaster so bad that even the ears of everyone who hears of it will tingle (II Kings 21:12). Because I am gracious, I gave Manasseh a message even closer to home. I told him that I was going to come in and scrub him like a plate on one side, turn him over, and scrub him on the other. Now, wouldn't that get your attention?   Manasseh's response was to put the prophet Isaiah in a log and cut him in half. Nice guy, huh?"

"Still, Father, You haven't answered my question. Why didn't you just destroy this king and save the people from what appeared to be devastating misery?"

"Yes, so many appeared to suffer. I could have changed the outcome, but that is not who I Am. I was seeking Manasseh's heart. There is nothing man can do that will keep Me from loving him. You will see. As Manasseh's consequences ensued, he found himself captured by the Assyrians who turned him over to Nebuchadnezzar. Israel's 10 tribes were wiped out, scattered. Only the two tribes of Judah remained, and they left. It was just as I had said.

"The Babylonians had a parade for Manasseh; only Nebuchadnezzar was the featured float, so to speak. Nebuchadnezzar was fully aware of the wealth and fame Manasseh had inherited, having sent envoys

during King Hezekiah's reign to inquire about his God, only to be shown the riches he had procured. Humiliating Manasseh would make Nebuchadnezzar even more powerful. He put a ring in his nose, and lead him down the main streets of Babylon in bronze shackles by a rope, like a cow.

"People on earth might say Manasseh got what he deserved. Here he was, king, leader of My people, thousands of Babylonians jeering him; oh, how they laughed and made fun. They even made fun of Me, Jesus. He did look pitiful, but I had not deserted him. There was more to come. Filthy, starving, covered in shackles, being led like a cow…right there on Main Street, Manasseh humbled himself before Me and prayed. Amidst the shrieking, frenzied, roaring crowd, he repented. A man who came in at the heights of spirituality and brought Judah down to the absolute lowest denominator…more wicked than the heathen nations he had conquered…what did I do to such a man? I forgave him. Not only that, I reinstated Manasseh on the throne, and he did good.

"Elohim created mankind. I hold My children in the palm of My hand and will never let them go. When My children make mistakes, I work with them and continually call them. They still suffer the consequences of their choices. Manasseh had a great undoing. He was the Hitler of his day; but, he was My own child and I forgave him.

"Father, how can You love a person as wicked as Manasseh? It hardly seems fair."

"Jesus, My love knows no end. You will see. I didn't desire that Manasseh suffer, but that was his choice. It was only in his suffering that he returned to

Me. Oh, I was so joyous to dwell with him again. Manasseh tried very hard to reestablish Jerusalem and the temple, and told the people that I was the God of Israel. Unfortunately, he had a son who became king and immediately reverted everything right back to the way if was before Manasseh's captivity. He was as evil as his father.

"Jesus, I pray the story of Manasseh reaches all people. I don't care what they have done, or what the Deceiver has told them, or how far they have fallen...I am Elohim, and I will never let them go. My greatest desire is that they turn to Me."

PRAYER: Elohim, if You didn't let go of Manasseh, I know you will never let go of me.

Further Study: II Kings 21,
II chronicles 33

MICAH

"*Father, You had some harsh words delivered to Israel through Your servant Micah. Why?*"

"**For centuries, I had gone through the ups and downs of My children of Israel. They continually were rejecting Me and following their own ways. Their own ways always led to disaster. I delivered them time after time. There comes a time when one must reap the consequences of his decisions. The time was drawing close for Israel.**

"**Because I care, I sent a devastating message to them. I told them how they had over and over turned their backs on Me. I reminded them of My promise to Abraham, how I had delivered them from Egypt, how I brought them to the Promised Land, and how I blessed them.**

"**I also pointed out how they had brought cruelty to their own people, how the rich were crushing the poor and taking advantage of them. They thought by bringing Me animal sacrifices, they could appease Me.**

"**The Assyrian Army was on the verge of wiping them out. I had to painfully be blunt with them, to save them from destruction! I told them I did not want the sacrifice of a 1000 rams. I did not want the sacrifice of year-old calves. I did not want 10,000 rivers of oil. I did not want their first born child.**

"**What I wanted from My children were three things:**

1. Do Justice

> *2. Show Mercy.*
> *3. Walk humbly with Me.*

"That's all I wanted from My children. I wanted them to show justice to the brothers and sisters; to treat others fairly. I wanted them to show mercy to all. And most important, I wanted them to walk with me with a thankful heart, listen, and share with Me. But the children would not listen, and they were destroyed by the Assyrians. I cried!!!"

PRAYER: Father, help me show justice and mercy and listen to You as I go on my journey.

Further Study: Micah 6:8

YAHWEH, I AM
THAT I AM

'*Father, I sing to You this song: a psalm of David:*

I waited patiently for the Lord;
He turned to me and heard my cry.
He lifted Me out of the slimy pit,
Out of the mud and mire;
He set my feet on a rock
And gave me a firm place to stand.
He put a new song in my mouth,
A hymn of praise to our God.
Many will see and fear the Lord
And put their trust in Him.

Blessed is the one
Who trusts in the Lord,
Who does not look to the proud,
To those who turn aside to false gods.
Many, Lord my God,
Are the wonders You have done,
The things You planned for us.
None can compare with You;
Were I to speak and tell of Your deeds,
They would be too many to declare.

Sacrifice and offering You did not desire…
But, my ears You have opened…

Burnt offerings and sin offerings You did not require.
Then I said, "Here I am, I have come…"
It is written about me in the scroll.
I desire to do Your will, my God;
Your law is within my heart.'

"Father, I have heard all of the stories We have gone over together. I know the depths of Your love for Me and for Your children. I must go and face the enemy. I know he will throw everything he has at Me. I know the religious leaders are hardened in their hearts and under Satan's influence. I know they will be threatened that they will lose their power and influences. Please go over Your assurance of Your presence with Me. Your beautiful name, YAHWEH, contains the sum total of Your promise to Me. I want to hear it again."

"Of all My names, this one embraces all I will be and do for You. This is one of the earliest names I used to describe Myself to My children. They were in a world which was largely controlled by the evil one, and of themselves they had no power to repulse him. As I introduced Myself to all of the leaders in the past, I always introduced Myself as 'YAHWEH, I AM THAT I AM.' Here I am, as the One who loves them, and as the only One who can defeat the words and actions of the serpent. I have all you will need."

"My heart is fully Yours, My Father. I trust You. Daily I will seek Your presence in My life in order that the world will see You reflected in all that I do, for knowing You is life eternal."

PRAYER: Thank You for the promise of being all I need. I accept You and trust You will work in me to will and do of Your pleasure.

Further Study: Psalms 40-42.

HOSEA

The Bible uses the term "God's Wrath" over and over again, but what exactly is God's wrath? Does the term seem inconsistent with His character? Have you ever attempted to explain God's wrath, only to be left feeling inept, incompetent? Well, let's see what God's wrath looks like in the Old Testament. The Book of Hosea dispels the confusion and paints a most beautiful picture of a compassionate God longing for the return of His wayward children, in this case the ten Northern tribes of Israel; but, in a broader view, us.

"My Father, You sent a strong message through the prophet Hosea that Israel was going to be wiped out by the Assyrians. Although this seems rather rash, it was Your last ditch effort to reach Your children, wasn't it, after years and years of pleading? At the time, they were doing everything You had commanded them. They kept the Sabbath. The sacrificial system was intact. They paid tithe. And yet, they knew nothing of You. How does that happen, Father? How could they take a tree, chop half of it for firewood, and worship the other half?" (Hosea 4:12).

"Doesn't make sense, does it, Jesus? Yes, in theory, they did look good; but, in fact, they knew nothing about worship, and they had no knowledge of Me. Have you noticed how earthly parents never stop loving their children, no matter what? I put that love in their hearts. It's the same love I have for My Children…undying love. Oh, how I loved Israel. I didn't desire sacrifices; I longed for relationships. Nothing else matters if I don't have their hearts, but

My people had given their hearts to another. My servant Hosea tried everything to try and get the people's attention and turn them around, but to no avail."

Through Hosea, God appeals to the children of Israel again and again. The first chapters of the book tell of God's explicit instructions to Hosea to marry Gomer, even though she would become unfaithful to him. Gomer gives Hosea a child, yet births two more children whom she infers are illegitimate. Eventually, she runs away and becomes a prostitute. Hosea longed for her and traveled to the big city…the "red light" district. Every evening he dragged himself up one street and down the next until he finally found her. Hosea is forced to purchase her freedom, which he does gladly; and then carries her home to rest and think.

"Holy Father, such a sad story. How could Hosea bring an adulteress home, one who had treated him cruelly, and then profess his love to her again? Why did You tell Hosea to go after her knowing her heart?"

"Jesus, everything I instructed Hosea to do was laden with meaning for those who would listen. His story is a love letter, really, to My children; a real-life parable of My endless love for Israel even after they did the same thing as Gomer, prostituting themselves with evil. As you know, there is simply nothing mankind can do to relinquish the everlasting love in My heart. It never dies. NEVER.

"I made one final plea for My people to come back to Me. I reminded them how I taught them to walk, how I brought them out of bondage, through the Red Sea, gave them manna…and yet they complained. The more I called, the more they went away (Hosea

11:2). I spoke to them like an earthly father, reminding them that when they were small, I did everything in the world I could do for them, literally holding them in My arms with love.   It made no difference whatsoever."

With an aching heart, God said, *"How can I give you up Ephraim? How can I hand you over Israel? (Hosea 11:8).* God longed to hold Israel in His arms again; but, He knew that Ephraim wanted to worship idols, and He had no choice but to acknowledge their decision. <u>That is "God's Wrath." He let them go.</u> There is nothing else He could do. He has to abide by their decisions.

"My dear Son, I cannot put into words the sadness that surrounds heaven when a soul loses his way; and, instead of turning to Me for help, walks deeper into darkness.   The Israelites had followed Satan's call again and again, until they could no longer hear My voice.

"You will tell the story of the prodigal son, Jesus. The daddy will have to let him go. There was nothing else he could do when the son asked for his inheritance. Oh, the heartache that the father felt. It's the same heartache I feel: Imagine anyone thinking I let a soul slip out of My hands because he or she didn't obey Me.   How can My children even think that? I wish people would see the evidence of My love all around them. You know, Jesus, I leave love notes everywhere for My beloved children to read, just hoping they will look up."

No one knows what goes on in another's inner life. Many struggle in silence, searching. When the gospel is shared, let it be about God's endless love, not about rules."

"Bring people to know Me."

PRAYER: Father I pray I will always love You and never run from You.

Further study: Book of Hosea,
Ephesians 11:1-8,
Romans 1,6,24-28

MOSES

What if God asked you to do something for which you felt totally incapable? Let's throw something crazy out there. What if God asked you to be His personal spokesperson to the King; and to complicate things, you stuttered! Well, that's just what He asked of his friend, Moses…a great story, by the way. Moses was reluctant to take the call, but he did. In the end, his greatest desire was not granted. Jesus had some questions about that for His Father.

"Father, I've been thinking about Moses this morning, and wondering why You didn't let him go into the Promised Land. I know that was his greatest desire."

"You know, Jesus, Moses is very special to Me. I waited over 430 years for such a leader to deliver My children Israel who were being held in slavery by the Egyptians. When Moses was born, Pharaoh had just ordered the killing of all Israelite boys under the age of two. How courageous and daring Moses' mother was to have Miriam place him in the Nile in a little basket boat. I shut Moses' mouth just like I would later shut the mouths of the lions in the Daniel story. I opened it again when Pharaoh's daughter came to the river, and Moses was raised in the very home of the man who had tried to kill him. As I said, a great story!"

"Father, already Moses had lost his family, and then he foolishly killed the Egyptian, causing him to run for his life. And then the children of Israel… they weren't an easy bunch to manage. After all that, it seems Moses could have received his reward."

"My Kingdom isn't about earthly rewards which are so fleeting. When Moses fled to the wilderness, where he remained for forty years, we got to know each other. He had much to learn after being raised in the King's palace. In the wilderness, he tended sheep…a great way to learn patience…and we talked. He was just the right man for the job, though he was not an easy man to convince! As Moses began to trust Me, his faith grew. During the 40 years of leading Israel through the wilderness, Moses trusted Me and always had the best interest of the Israelites at heart.

"There was a time when Moses was speaking with Me up on the mountain. We had been together forty days. Do you see the repetition, Jesus? Forty days, forty years…I use that number quite often. Anyway, I told Moses that the children of Israel were worshipping a golden calf, and I thought perhaps I would destroy them and start all over.

"Moses' response was immediate and quite interesting. He told Me, that I couldn't do that! He had his reasons. I listened while he presented his case, all the while thinking how wonderful our relationship was, how We could openly communicate with each other like that. I desire that in every relationship with My children.

"I gave Israel every tangible experience I could think of to show them how much I loved them. Did you know, Jesus, they were only eleven days away from the Red Sea and going into the Promised Land…11 DAYS! Because of their stubbornness, however, eleven days took forty years! Moses finally lost patience one day…so out of character for him. We had spoken earlier about how to provide water for

the people and animals; but, in anger, he disregarded My words and took matters into his own hands. His actions both disappointed and dishonored Me. He was only human, and I understood; but sin always has consequences. If My children only knew how much I hate sin."

"Father, when I look at the ways in which You provided for Your children over and over again, their behavior is puzzling. How could Israel choose idols over You? Just puzzling!"

" I give My children a choice. Love must come from the heart. Because I loved Moses so very much, and so appreciated his work on My behalf, I took him to Mount Nebo and let him see the Promised Land that he would never enter. We had such a great lifetime together, Moses and I, that when he died, I missed him. To tell you the truth, Jesus, I always had greater plans for Moses. I wanted to bring him to the real Promised Land. And so I did."

"Father, I admire Moses and I certainly look forward to the day that I can meet him."

"You know, Jesus, you will meet Moses; and that day might come sooner than you think."

PRAYER: Father, thank You for wanting me to be in the Promised Land with You… forever.

Further Study: Deuteronomy 6, 8, 19

NAHUM

"*Father, why did You have Nahum draw such a harsh description of what You are like?*"

"**I can see why You would ask that question.**"

"*He paints You as jealous, wrathful, and vengeful. Nahum used very harsh words about You, but I know You are different. I know You as a loving Father holding Your children in Your arms, One who clothes His Children and loves them with an everlasting love.*"

"**I always want the very best for My children. I have great plans for My children, but sometimes they have their own plans. They want to do what they want. They want to follow their own desires. I had to recognize My children's choices and take a step back. And when I step back they have consequences for the decisions they make.**

"**The northern tribes of Israel had decided they wanted nothing to do with Me. This broke My heart. I sent seven prophets to try to draw them back to Me, but My children did not listen to them. Jesus, I finally had to honor their decision to separate themselves from Me. Their decision had consequences.**"

"*Father, why Nahum?*"

"**I sent My prophet Nahum with a very strong message to My children. It was My last chance to get their attention, and sometimes I can only do that with a harsh message. I care for My children and meet them where they are. I didn't want to send a message** *with harsh words. I wanted them to know that what they were doing would lead to their destruction. Nahum told them that desertion was coming to the ten tribes. I wanted to prevent that, but the people would not listen. That was not the way I wanted to speak to My children. They had 28 years to ponder Nahum's message, but they would not listen. Sadly, the Assyrians came and destroyed them and they were scattered all over the earth. What I want You to understand from Nahum is that I sent him to the people, My children, because I wanted the very best for them. I wanted to remind My children not to wander from Me, and that I would pursue them to bring them back into a relationship with Me. My wrath was respecting their decisions. I simply had to step back and say there was nothing more I could do. I cried."*

"Father, I can see the pain You still have. I will show the people how much You love them, and rather than screaming at them as You did with Nahum, You would rather speak to them in a still, small voice as You did with Elijah."

PRAYER: Father, may I always listen to your quiet, still voice.

Further Study: Book of Nahum

FACE TO FACE
WITH THE ENEMY

"*Father, there is great joy being in Your presence again after having been in this dark earth. I have known from the foundation of the world this moment would come. I feel the darkness of this earth begin to enfold Me and the glory of Your presence is growing dimmer. I know You and the Holy Spirit will be with Me. Because of the love that binds us together, I am willing to go to Our children to seek and save them.*"

"**Son, I will be with You as You walk among Our children; even though You will walk through the valley of the shadow of death, I will comfort You. The Prince of darkness is in counsel with members who were once reflectors of that glory from being in My presence, but are now full of darkness, their beings reflecting the ravages sin has upon them. They know their conduct is leading them to their destiny with death; unless…unless they can devise a plan to crush You, the Messenger. They cannot pierce the light surrounding them. They are desperate!**

"**The agenda for this fiendish counsel was to devise ways to crush You, My Son. It was their only hope of extending their so-called kingdom, that kingdom that existed in the hearts of men and women who fell prey to their lies. Yet all of those demons knew in their heart there was still some connection between heaven and earth. They knew there was a desire placed in man's heart for something beyond the darkness and woe of earth. They also realized that** *when man yielded to that desire, and sought Me, there was a power to resist their lies; they lost control of those men. They desire to snuff out the flame of Your presence and man's power to resist their evil influence. All throughout Your life the Prince of darkness found no way to cause You to distrust Me. He knows he has to find a way, or...*

"*Son, remember the time Lucifer made his fatal choice to start this controversy in the beginning? We stood face to face, both of us had tears streaming down our cheeks. His tears were from begging to be restored to his former position. All beings in heaven, both the unfallen and those who followed the deceivers' lies, were listening to hear the reason for the tears coming from the eyes of the Majesty of Heaven. I painfully said, 'no, it is too late; you have gone too far'. But this once mighty angel said, 'Why? You have forgiven and reinstated me before, what difference does one more time make?'*

"*I could not force him to obey, that would only create a rebel. My willingness to forgive would not change his heart; it was not forgiveness he needed. He needed healing. Sin leaves one wounded and sick, and it calls for healing. But he had gone too far; he'd lost the desire and the capacity to grasp truth. Without that, he would only continue in his downward path. I had to let him go. I had to leave him to himself. I was powerless to bring him back. Only by love is love awakened and, he repelled My love over and over. My love did not draw him; he couldn't respond to it any more. I had to let him go.*

"*My Son, Satan is considering his options. He knows You will have been without food or drink for forty days and that You will be famished. Satan questions how you can continue to believe in Me, a Father Who would allow His Son to languish in this god-forsaken place. Satan will think that in Your weakened state, You will not be able to resist his implication that You cannot trust Your Father. He believes in his heart, if he fails to get You not to trust, he will be doomed.*

"My Son, the master of deceit assured himself that as he approached Eve and Adam in the beginning, he would use a disguise. He will present himself as an angel of light, sent from his father to nurture You back to health. He will tell You 'I need to know if You are the One sent from God because there is a fallen angel present on earth, pretending to be the Messiah.' He will try to lower Your defenses by making You think he is the faithful servant, just making sure he is doing his job. He will try to force You to prove to him Who You are by producing a miracle that You are the Son of God."

"This plan is perfect!" Satan thought to himself, and he shouted out to his followers, "That's it! That's perfect! I've got Him! Jesus will fail to rely on the evidence He has accumulated throughout His life, and will think He has to show me a miracle to convince me Who He is. Then I've got Him. He will have to do something beyond what man can do, showing it's not the love of the Father that enables Him, but His own power."

"Satan is very satisfied with his plan. He feels confident he can show to the entire universe that he truly is the lord of this planet earth. He believes if he gets You to perform a miracle, then it's not My love for You that enables You, but Your own power. He wants

to portray Me as arbitrary, demanding, and unforgiving. He thinks I will have to concede and allow him back into heaven."

"Father, I know Your love for Me and Your children. You have always drawn Me into Your love. There is always joy in Your presence."

PRAYER: Oh, Father, thank You for the evidence of Your love for me, and that You have not abandoned me to the lies of the deceiver.

Further study:
Isaiah 14
Ezekiel 28
Matthew 4:1-12
Mark 1:12-14
Luke 4:1-13

HOW TO HAVE VICTORY OVER THE DECEIVER- PART ONE

"*Oh, the darkness!*" Jesus thought as He adjusted to the absence of the light of heaven. "*The warmth and light in My Father's presence are so comforting. But the darkness of this earth is not nearly as disturbing as the darkness of man's heart. The glory and beauty of My Father's love has almost been extinguished from their hearts by the religious leaders.*" In a firm, determined voice He said to Himself, "*I must be about My Father's business and demonstrate for them what My Father really is like.*"

Lying in the dirt, with rocks strewn all around Him, He felt the horrible pain of the lack of food and water. He noticed in the sky the vultures circling above Him, waiting for the passing of their prey. He was not alone in the desert. He knew of the wider perspective He just came from. The eyes of every being in the universe were focusing intently on this scene. He recalled the words spoken by the prophet Isaiah, who had been shown this scene centuries before. He wrote, "Just as many were astonished at Him…His appearance was marred more than any man, and His form more than the sons of men." He felt that in His body; it was suffering from the lack of food and water for nearly forty days.

All the unseen fallen angels were there also. But they were observing their leader, Lucifer, who once stood by the throne of God. He, too, was watching Jesus. He knew

Jesus was at the point of death. This serpent was waiting for the exact moment of Jesus' greatest weakness, then he would strike!

The moment arrived. This angel of darkness transformed himself into an angel of light. He heard Jesus' prayer to His Father for help; and in that prayer He heard Him say, *"Not My will, but Thy will be done."* So he approached Jesus, posing as a messenger sent from heaven in answer to His prayer. The Devil recalled when he had once approached Eve in the Garden using the disguise of a serpent. That worked, so he will do it again, but this time disguised as an angel sent by God. He could hide the exterior, but he could not hide his heart of hate and darkness.

All beings of heaven, and the angels of darkness, recalled the previous meeting of Jesus and Satan. Then it was the Mighty God meeting with a beautiful angel of light. They saw tears flowing from the eyes of the Majesty of heaven, and heard the pathos in His voice, pleading with His friend to turn from his path of darkness and death, but to no avail. Jesus had no choice but to banish him and his cohorts from heaven. The first phase of this great controversy had past.

What a drastic change in scenery in this second meeting. They once stood on the sea of glass. Now they are in the desert, marred by a thousand years of the devastation of sin. While on the sea of glass it was the Mighty God standing before the angel of light, appealing to him to return. Now it is the mighty angel of darkness, wrapped in false light, standing over the emaciated body lying in the dirt. He had to use every weapon of hell to destroy Jesus.

All of the witnesses of this encounter were waiting with

bated breath to hear the words artfully chosen by the Devil. The Deceiver had hoped that the light would bedazzle the Lord, and that He would believe His loving Father in heaven was sending relief. The Devil knew he had to get Jesus to use His own power to relieve Himself from the hunger and thirst, thus showing that Jesus could not withstand him as a man. He thought, "Now I can show that God is a liar. It is not sin which kills, it is the Lord Who leaves His children to languish, and He kills those who disobey Him." The Devil determined that he must get Jesus to perform this miracle for Himself; then he could claim he won the great controversy.

Jesus knew He was picking up where Adam and Eve left off. He also knew that in the heart of every man in the past, and every man coming into this world, each would have to personally face this controversy in his heart. Jesus, at the point of death, could not yield to the deception of the Devil.

The Devil could hide his exterior, but he could not hide the darkness, jealousy, and hate in his heart. For out of the depth of his wicked heart came the lie, "I have been sent to help You", he said. "I must make sure You are the Son of God." Insinuating, "God would never allow His Son to be in this condition, and I don't want to feed the enemy." He hoped he could lead Jesus to doubt He was God's Son, and to prove it to the Devil. He went on, "Make these stones, which already look like a loaf of bread, into real bread. Your Father would want You to do it in order to prove Who You are."

Jesus could not deny the evidence of God in His life, and He still had echoing in His ears the statement made by His Father at the baptism; ***"This is My beloved Son, in Whom I am well pleased."***

Therefore, He used the only tools given to all men: the Word of God, the evidence of God in the world around him, and the evidence of His Father in His life. Jesus quickly picked up on the deception. He used the very words spoken to Moses in the wilderness after having been supplied with the manna for Israel. "And He humbled you and let you be hungry, and fed you with manna which you did not know, nor did your fathers know, that He might make you understand that man does not live by bread alone, but man lives by everything that proceeds out of the mouth of the LORD."

"Now I see what it is!" The Devil angrily shouted to his followers, "I knew there was a power available to all men to overcome my plans, and to keep man in connection with heaven. He used the words of Scripture! I must change my plans, and force Him to prove Who He is another way."

PRAYER: Father, thank You for providing a way for me to overcome whenever I am tempted. And, thank You, that the way to keep me in touch with You through Your Word, is so simple.

Further Study:
Matthew 4:1-11
Mark 1:9-13
Luke 4:1-13

HOW TO HAVE VICTORY OVER THE DECEIVER- PART TWO

"The angels in heaven were fixed on the terrible ordeal Jesus was going through. They urgently wanted to rush to Jesus' aid. They turned toward their Father hoping to present their request to rescue their beloved Friend and Master. But when they looked at the Father to see His reaction, they were shocked. They saw He was in agony. Tears were streaming down His face. He had turned His face from the horrible scene, almost like He could not bear what He was witnessing. The angels assumed they were the ones hurting over what Jesus was enduring – but the Father?! They were thinking, "How could the Majesty of the entire universe, the all-powerful God, appear to be helpless? How could He be in such pain? Why does He not take action?"

The mighty angels were moved with compassion. Many of them drew nearer to the Father to comfort Him. They had to admit they were confused once again. Ever since this great conflict between God and Satan had begun, each Member of the Godhead had often acted in ways they could not understand. At times They had allowed the angels to minister to men, then at times they were restrained from assisting them.

It seemed to the angelic host that justice had to be taken in reaction to sin. They saw what happened when Satan and his followers were banished from heaven. They witnessed what appeared to be justice when Adam and Eve were removed from Eden. The flood and Sodom and Gomorrah were times of justice. And now, letting His own Son confront the Devil by Himself?

What they had not yet realized was that this great conflict was being allowed to be played out for the angels to witness. They, along with all men, had to understand that Satan's slanderous assertions against God's character had to be addressed and answered. But God could not just explain to them what would happen. Words can be cheap. Actions really define character. God had to let all see the result of distrust.

Satan spoke a lie to Adam and Eve. He had told them, "If you distrust God's orders to refrain from eating from the tree of good and evil, you won't die. God is just afraid you will become like Him, knowing good and evil. I know, because He did that to me in heaven. He cast me out. You can't trust Him."

What they did not understand is that obedience can only be in response to love. To use might, power, and force to get one to obey only creates rebellion, and eventually creates a devil. God cast Satan out, He did not destroy him. God was in a bind. He could not have allowed the natural consequences of sin and rebellion to have its effect at that time; it would have created fear and distrust among the angels. The great conflict had to be played out so that all could know that the natural results of sin is death. Sin carries its own consequence. God does not kill. His universe has to be operated on the basis of love. God was trying to keep man from destroying himself.

No human eye witnessed this scene in the desert; this was allowed to be carried out for the entire universe to see. The angelic host saw the furious reaction of the Devil when he could not get this weak, emaciated Being to yield to his suggestion. There was a pause in the drama. The angels saw the serpent regain his composure, and then move in closer to strike again.

The angels watched the impostor sweep Jesus up in his arms, and bear Him to the highest place in the temple courtyard. The Devil thought, "Oh, You want to use the Word to protect Yourself, I can also use it." The Devil used a verse right out of the Scriptures and said, "If You are the Son of God, Throw Yourself down, for it is written, 'He will give His angels charge concerning You; and on their hands they will bear You up, lest You strike Your foot against a stone.'"

The angelic host looked to the Father, waiting for just one word from Him to rescue His Son. But again, God acted strangely. He did not give the command, and He did not interfere. God had to let the angels see that man, in his weakest form, could withstand the Devil by using His Word.

The Devil knew Jesus had been exposed to the Jewish belief that when the Messiah would come, they would know it was truly Him, because He would go to the highest point in the temple, and cast himself down, and not be harmed because the angels would protect Him, thus proving He was the Son of God,

The angels were restless, for now the Devil was questioning their fidelity to God. He was tempting them to take things in their own hands and prove their loyalty to their Master. They looked to the Father, waiting for His bidding, but He never bade them go.

They then heard the voice of Jesus, *"On the other hand, it is written, 'You shall not put the Lord your God to the test.'"*

Once again, the angels saw the Devil recoil in anger; he

was powerless before their Lord. "It can't be that simple," the angels thought, "the most feeble person can withstand the Devil's greatest temptations by using the Word of the Lord.

PRAYER: Oh, Mighty, Powerful, Loving Lord, thank You for the evidence of Your love for me. Thank You for showing me that I can prevail against any trial, as long as I put my trust in You and Your Word. Help me to store Your promises away in my heart that I might not abandon my trust in You.

Further Study:
Matthew 4:1-11
Mark 1:9-13
Luke 4:1-13

HOW TO HAVE VICTORY OVER THE DECEIVER- PART THREE

Twice the foe tempted Jesus to doubt Who He was, and to prove He was the Son of God, and twice he was defeated. Now the mask is off. No longer can Satan hide under the deception that he is an angel sent from God. Fully unmasked, he now stands before the Son of the Most High God. This time the brilliant glory is hidden from him, but the fact God is the God of love shined through, making the Devil shrink back in fear.

The Devil now changes his strategy. He still has one more deception in his bag to cause Jesus to fail. He says to himself, "I know You have come to win the world back to You and Your Father. You have not fallen for my first two attempts. So I will not try to fool You; You are too sharp for me. You win! I give up. There is no need to go through whatever You are doing. I surrender. You can have the dominion of the earth back without a struggle. You can go back to Your Father claiming victory."

Then the Devil causes to pass before Jesus all the cities of the world. Like a swindler, selling to a gullible man his fools gold, he causes the scene of the world to glitter before His eyes. The Devil sweeps his hand across the brilliant scene and says, "All of this is Yours, and I have the right and power to give it to You, if You will just acknowledge me as the lord of this earth. Just bow in recognition of this, and You win the controversy, and I give up."

He continued with all of his persuasive ability to allure Jesus from His mission. "It will be so much easier for You; You can have it without a struggle."

The Deceiver was not ignorant of the Messiah's coming. He had studied the Scriptures for centuries. He could not imagine who would come, and he was shocked when he realized it was Jesus. "How could He have given up Who He was, and what He left behind, to come to this dark earth to redeem these worthless creatures? Surely He could not love them that much," he thought. He reasoned, "Maybe the dazzling world I pass before Him, coupled with the agony He has gone through so far, will appeal to Him to accomplish His goal another way."

Jesus would not bargain with the enemy. He declared in a firm, loud voice, *"Be gone, Satan! For it is written, 'You shall worship the Lord Our God, and serve Him only.'"*

As the glory of the Father's glory faded, the darkness of the world and the barrenness of the desert set in. Jesus was lying in the sand, weak and emaciated when the serpent struck. All heaven watched the face to face encounter. They witnessed their beloved Commander, as that snake bit His heal. Jesus administered three mighty blows to the head of that serpent, marking the beginning of the end of the deceiver.

In heaven the angels looked to their Father, and with a smile, He nods toward them; now, they can go and minster to Jesus! With great joy, some of them rushed to the side of Jesus, and nurtured Him back to health. They said to Him, "Your Father suffered with You and He was so happy how You vanquished the Devil. He is well pleased with You."

Jesus knew the Devil had no idea what His mission was. Jesus had to face every temptation man faced in the beginning in order to reveal that man could overcome the Devil in the same manner He had.

Jesus also knew coming into this world to redeem His children would cause all the gates of hell to burst open, and the very ones He came to save would use all the weapons of hell to kill Him. That's just what sin does to a heart not yielded to God. For the Word says, "He came to His own, and His own received Him not."

Jesus also knew He was not coming into this world to get man to stop sinning. All sin is a natural result flowing from a heart which does not put his trust in the Father.

One of the main questions all the beings in heaven had was, "What is God like when He comes into the presence of sin and sinners; how will He treat them? Truly, what is the character of God like?"

When Jesus was strengthened by the angels, they all hugged Him as He began to start His mission. He turned and faced the direction in which He entered the desert. He spoke to the angels over His shoulder as He began to walk away, *"I must be about My Father's business, to seek and save all who will come unto Me, in order that I might restore them to be the sons of God."*

PRAYER: Father, thank You for sending Your Son. Thank You that He was willing to come and find me. Thank You that You have sent Your Sweet Holy Spirit to comfort and restore me into Your Son's image. I surrender my heart to You, in order that You, Your Son, and the Holy Spirit may make Your home within me.

Further Study:
Matthew 4:1-11
Mark 1:9-13
Luke 4:1-13

AFTERGLOW

Thank you for going with us on this journey. Now that you have heard a host of testimonies from those in the Scriptures, it is our prayer that you have a similar response to this revelation about your Father, His Son Jesus, and the Holy Spirit. Run among the people, face all aglow, and tell them about what you have discovered.

Please don't let this cause your journey to slow down or end. We hope you have had a chance to see how all Scripture reveals the heart of God. Continue reading, and take Him with you by asking Him to reveal Himself to you.

May our testimony be that of the two men running back to Jerusalem late at night after having encountered Jesus on the road; "Didn't our heart burn within us as we walked with Him in the way."

ABOUT
THE AUTHORS

Ernie Pyle was born in 1944 in El Paso Texas. He was reared in a Christian home. He accepted Jesus Christ and the Love of His Heavenly Father, and was baptized at the age of 13.

Ernie's career included owning his own business, national sales trainer for 3 corporations, but the height of his professions was as a Pastor.

In 2008 Ernie and Rob co-founded "Knowing God Ministries". They specialize in the Hebrew Names of God. They led over 70 seminars in the United States and Canada.

Ernie lost his precious Sue in 2019. He is currently retired and tending to his 8 herd of cattle. (Ernst, Ernesto, Suzy-cue, Ernestine, Sue-Sue, Big E, Little E, Susie, E Junior)

Ernie and Rob currently co-teach a bible class at their church in Arlington Texas

William "Rob" Sheppard considers his greatest goal in life is to understand the character of his Heavenly Father. Two events led to that goal.

Born and raised in the Pacific Northwest, his passion was to be a logger, and to ultimately be an operator of a D9 caterpillar. That all changed the day his daughter was born. He was home alone wondering about being a father, and what he could give his new baby. For the first time in he began watching a preacher and by the end of the sermon he was inviting Jesus into his life.

The second event occurred while in college when he took a class titled, "The Names of God."   His new quest was to find the answer to the question, "What does this tell me about my Father's character?

The discoveries he made as a result of asking that question have impacted his studies, his messages as a pastor for seven years, his lectures as a university teacher for thirteen years, and his ongoing ministry as a professional counselor.

Together with Ernie Pyle, a ministry named "Knowing God Ministries" was founded. The goal of that ministry is to tell others about the character of God and His unconditional love for all.